Our Stories, Their Stories

Captured Moments of Canadian History Gifted to Us by Canadian Seniors

Created and Edited by Natalie Fraser
on behalf of HelpAge Canada

Library and Archives Canada Cataloguing in Publication

Our stories, their stories : captured moments of Canadian history gifted to us by Canadian seniors / edited by Natalie Fraser.

Issued in print and electronic formats.
ISBN 978-0-9811504-6-8 (pbk.).--ISBN 978-0-9869413-9-9 (pdf)

1. Older people--Canada--Biography. I. Fraser, Natalie, 1972-, editor

HQ1060.5.O97 2014 305.26092'271 C2014-907567-7
C2014-907568-5

Published by Sassy Sunflower Books, Ottawa ON, Canada

Acknowledgements

Thank you so much to all the Canadian seniors who contributed their stories to this wonderful project. I would also like to pay thanks to ***HelpAge Canada***'s first student Ambassador Kelsie Winsor, a young coop high school student who has helped by typing in stories, my step daughter Coco-Simone Finken for volunteering her expertise on the design of the cover for this first edition. Additionally, I pay thanks to the volunteer services of my mother Janet Beers (Standish), a retired English teacher who has done her fair share of red pen projects and really was my co-editor on this project, and my husband, Kirk Finken, an editor and writer, for his assistance in the editing of this book.

Foreword

My grandmother is one of my best friends, as is my mother, and both of them have pieces of our history in this book. Three years ago a student of mine suggested this job at ***HelpAge Canada*** to me and because of my love for the seniors in my life I pursued and got this job.

In the time I have been with this amazing organization, I have met so many diverse seniors with so many interesting stories that were not being documented. I had heard from many of those story tellers that their stories didn't matter or that they had written or told them for themselves and family only. From my perspective, these stories were Canadian history being lost. The stories needed and deserved to be captured and to be handed on to future generations. So I put forth a proposal to spend one year gathering stories from Canadian seniors about their Canadian experiences.

This book shares our national diversity and uniquely Canadian flare. There are stories of immigration, war, times in history, specific places at specific times, and rituals of the past that can be recognized by many and appreciated by all. As you journey through this book, sampling stories, remember they are all true. Enjoy them all and pay them forward to those you love and know.

Do You Have a Story to Tell?

I first got the idea for the ***HelpAge Canada*** *Our Stories, Their Stories* senior's project in the summer of 2013. By September of that year, we started reaching out to local Canadian seniors. The objective was to gather stories for one year and then publish them as a fund-raiser for ***HelpAge Canada***. By September 2014 we realized that this was so important and there was so much interest, with stories coming in from all over Canada, that this would be the premier edition, not the only one.

We are now taking stories for the Volume 2 of *Our Stories, Their Stories* which is schedule to come out in 2015. If you are inclined, send me a story of your own or from one of the elders in your life and pass it in for next year's publication. I know the stories that I gather from my family, give me a sense of belonging. Reading all these new stories gives me a proud rooted feeling of being lucky to be Canadian and proud to be part of our global village. The authors in this book helped build define and protect this country. ***HelpAge Canada*** is doing their part to help locally and globally. They are using the proceeds from these books to help seniors in Canada and all over the world live comfortable, safe and dignified lives.

Natalie Fraser
Local Programs Director at HelpAge Canada
Developer and Chief Editor
www.helpagecanada.ca

HelpAge Canada was founded in 1975 under the name *Help the Aged (Canada)* by a group of volunteers who were concerned that no Canadian charitable organization represented the interests and needs of older persons in Canada and in the developing world.

HelpAge Canada was one of the six founding organizations of ***HelpAge International***, a global network of over 80 organizations that help thousands of older people every day.

In 2010, *Help the Aged (Canada)* adopted its current name and look to match that of ***HelpAge*** International, and other ***HelpAge*** affiliates. ***HelpAge's*** mission is to work in partnership with other organizations to improve and maintain the quality of life of vulnerable older persons and their communities. Our vision at ***HelpAge*** is for older persons to lead secure, healthy, active and dignified lives.

We work with our partners to ensure that people everywhere understand how much older persons contribute to society and to protect their right to healthcare, social services, and economic and physical security.

In Canada

In Canada we focus on vulnerable and isolated seniors. We sparked the creation and support the work of the Nunavut Seniors Society, the first organization representing seniors in this immense Arctic region. ***HelpAge Canada*** has launched and continues to run programs that raise awareness and combat isolation in the Ottawa and Quebec City areas. Over the next few years, we will be continuing to expand our work across Canada.

Outside Canada

We provide assistance and empowerment to older persons in nine countries (Jamaica, Haiti, Grenada, Dominica, Democratic Republic of Congo, Kenya, India, Sri Lanka and the Philippines). We do this through:

- Sponsorship of grandparents, victims of sexual violence, retired advocates and members of marginalized communities
- Income generating activities
- Supporting emergency relief and reconstruction work in areas affected by disaster or conflict.

We believe that "age helps"—a position that puts the experience of older women and men at the center of our work.

For information, see *How You Can Help* on page 233.

Contents

War Stories

Depression Era

The Value of Community

Learning Skills

Oh, How Things Have Changed

Time Travel

Timeless

Captured Moments

Poems

Immigration

The Move of My Life

by Giselle Braeuel

It all started in Germany a long time ago at a party, one night in August of 1954. When I saw this young man walk into the room, tanned, tall and very good looking, I said to my father, who was there as well, "Look at HIM, that's the fellow I am going to marry!" My poor dad, being used to his crazy daughter, just replied, "Stop your nonsense, will you?"

It turned out that Hans had left for Canada two years earlier, and he was just back for a vacation to visit his mother.

Six weeks later I was sailing to Canada, a married woman, on a ship called *The Arosa Culm*. I was just beginning to realize the enormous step I had taken, a giant step from a life in a small town, surrounded by a close and very loving family.

I was sobbing my heart out! How tactless of me. My poor husband, who turned out to be a wonderful companion for the rest of his life, was very upset. "What's wrong with you?" he kept asking in desperation. I did love him dearly, of course, but after overcoming my parents' first vehement objections, then the rush with very hectic wedding preparations, the possible consequences of this enormous step suddenly dawned on me. But it was too late to change my mind.

Eleven days on the Atlantic Ocean, in October, on a boat which wasn't stabilized in those days, made for a very rough passage. I was too nauseated to eat or to show much affection to my husband. My thoughts changed from the initial excitement to dread. There would be another language, another culture and this huge city of Toronto was awaiting me.

Not only that, I would be expected to keep house! Living in my family's household and working in my father's stores, I had never cooked a meal in my life. My husband, 10 years older, "a man of the world", why on earth had he married Me? Why had I followed him? When would I see my family and friends again? Flying was frightfully expensive in those days, as were phone calls.

Then came land in sight, first the St. Lawrence River and a bit later Quebec City. It was an awesome feeling indeed as I stood at sundown on the ship's deck, my husband's arm tightly around my shoulder.

It was October, the trees were bare, a cold wind was already blowing, foreboding a winter as I had never experienced before. As we disembarked many passengers were carried off the boat on stretchers. A bus took us to the station where we boarded a train to Toronto.

Yes, it certainly took a while to adjust, but only a little while. I slowly stopped comparing everything to my hometown. As I got used to the language, I was able to communicate better and better. I was thrilled to meet people from different nationalities and all walks of life, and my horizon began to expand like a pancake after you put some baking powder into the batter. I loved the lakes! I found an interesting job in a commercial photo studio.

Toronto, although still far from what it offers today, had great cultural variety. However, I did miss the German Weinstuben and the cozy pubs, and I did find those beer joints with different entrances for men and women absolutely dreadful. Financially, too, times were a little rough, and for six years my husband worked, as well as studied, at night.

When my first son was born, of course, I did miss my family very much. There is a benefit to living through times like that which the philosopher F. Nietsche expressed well: "That which doesn't kill you, makes you stronger!"

When I went home for my first visit after three years, my parents' first grandchild in my arms, it was a wonderful reunion. But you know what? To say good-bye again after a few weeks didn't hurt anymore. Of course, as a first generation immigrant you somehow do forever put yourself "between two chairs" as the saying goes. But that's okay.

I belong to both worlds, and I find it enriching. Our sons feel at home in each country as well. They both turned out to be highly accomplished, and each of them is "making a difference". Advances in technology, like skyping, for instance, allow me to be as close to some friends and my siblings in Germany as if I had never left. I am spending the last phase of my life as a widow, but in great contentment, never looking back. What more can a person ask for?

The move of my life did take guts, but I never, ever had any regrets.

A Strong Lineage

by Patricia Stockwell

My maternal grandmother, Flora Pope, was in her own words, a true survivor. As a child, I often sat cuddled up to her side as she told and re-told stories of growing up in Guildford, England, south of London. One day, we were looking at a picture of the Guildford Castle, built in 1092 by William the Conquerer. I remember her words:

"We used to play here, my brothers and sisters and I. I was the youngest of nine children and my mother died giving birth to me. Her name was Harriet Karnzu and I always pretended that she had been a gypsy since her name sounded so foreign. My older brothers and sisters had to go to work every day, so I was left alone in my crib with soiled diapers until the neighbour woman discovered my plight and came to look after me. She eventually married my father and became my step-mother. Thank the Lord for that woman. I guess I was born a survivor. Lord knows, I've had to survive plenty of hard times in my life."

Then, she took out a picture of the grand old clock tower in Waterloo Station, London, England. She continued her story:

"Dearie, this is where I waited for Mrs. Burford of the Burford Coat Company to come and fetch me. I was 19 and I was to become the upstairs maid in their grand house in London. I was out in the world on my own for the first time. I had never been outside of Guildford before but I had longed to live in London with its shops and museums and theatres. I was engaged to be married before I took this trip but I caught the scoundrel cheating on me. I didn't give the ring back when he asked for it. Instead, I pawned it and bought the train ticket to London after I had answered Mrs Burford's advertisement in the London Times. It was in that Burford mansion that I met Lilly, the downstairs maid and William, the gardener. Lilly and William and I had some grand times together. Lilly and I wrote to each other after I came to Canada up until the time she died at the age of 92 and as you know, William and I got married just before the First World War. He was called into the service just one week after we were married. I missed him something awful and I worried about him all the time until he returned safe and sound at the end of the war. He was a survivor too, I guess."

I asked, "When did you come to Canada?" I knew the answer. I had heard the stories over and over but I wanted to hear her tell it once again.

"Patty, dear, we came to Canada in 1928 just before the Great Depression. There were no jobs in England after the war with so many men returning from war and competing for jobs. We had relatives in Brandon, Manitoba so we embarked on the long ocean voyage. We couldn't afford a suite so we were in steerage. The crowding and the stench was awful and I was sea-sick nearly the whole voyage. It took three weeks to make the trip and another week to travel by train from Montreal to Winnipeg. We certainly had some hard times in Manitoba. We were sharecropping on my brother's farm and of course we knew nothing about farming, both of us being city folks.

We lost what little money we did make during the Depression of the 30s. My sister, Gert, wrote and suggested we come to Southwestern Ontario where at least the weather was better. She was living in Kingsville at the time and she found us jobs at the huge Walker Farms in Walkerville, Ontario near Windsor. William was in charge of the horse barns where they raised their winning race horses and I was the housekeeper in the main house."

This was the hard part of the story. I clung to her arm as she continued:

"I told him not to go out that night. The roads were icy and the snow was falling but he would not listen. No. He loved his Thursday night card game with his cronies. I remember when the policeman came to the door. William had been waiting to cross by the train tracks when a train approached. A Model A came from the other direction, skidded and struck William, pushing him under the train. The policeman didn't want to tell me that he had been decapitated. We had a closed casket and I couldn't even see his beautiful face to say goodbye properly. By then, your Aunt Gwen was twelve, Judy was ten, your mom was eight and little Walter was four. I didn't know what I was going to do. I didn't want to stay in that house so Gert found us a house in Kingsville. I don't know how I survived those days but I managed to put food on the table by taking in laundry, keeping house for the rich Americans down by the lake and the odd stint at the Heinz factory in the summer."

Often, as an adult, I would remember those stories and I would dream of my grandmother and grandfather. I see them holding hands in bed in the dark, back in the Manitoba days, and I picture my grandmother, after his death, staring at William's picture late into the night after the children had gone to bed. I would wake up thinking that I was proud to come from such a strong lineage.

My Yellow Canadian Green Card

by Mina Azad

Immigration is somewhat like an arranged marriage. In my case, I married a country—without having a chance to peek at my future home land.

In May 1979, after graduating from the University of Michigan I found a one year employment with a university affiliate. A few months later, I convinced my employer to get me a U.S. "Green Card". The first step was to obtain a Labor Certificate. A few months later, there was an attack on the U.S. embassy in Tehran and American diplomats were taken hostage. There was no point in filing my Labor Certificate application until the "crisis" was over.

"Crisis" sounded too strong a word at that time. After all, in Iran such incidents were unprecedented. I expected a speedy release of the hostages and agreed to delay the application. So much for my optimism! Thanksgiving and Christmas holidays came and passed but the hostages remained in captivity.

As the hostage crisis prolonged my hopes for obtaining permanent residency declined. The end of my one year employment was approaching fast and I was faced to choose between two unwanted options: returning to Iran in the midst of a seemingly never ending political turmoil or staying in the U.S. on a no re-entry temporary permit.

Shortly after Christmas, I spoke with a friend who had contacts in a software contracting firm in Canada. Those days, Canada was on office automation high gears, mainframe computers had become the backbone of the financial and public sectors, database technology was at its infancy, and any little enhancement was considered a major upgrade. My software programming skills were in high demand.

I sent my resume and waited anxiously for an offer of a temporary one-year job in Canada. In early March, I got a preliminary verbal job offer that I accepted with no hesitation. The final offer was pending immigration approval which I presumed meaning a temporary work permit. A couple of weeks later I received a large package containing the job offer and a "Landed Immigrant" application. I filled the application and mailed it to Ottawa, Ontario, Canada.

In April, 1980, I received a letter instructing me to go for an interview with the Canadian consulate in Detroit. This was in the midst of the hostage crisis and I had psyched myself up for an unsuccessful short and stern interview at a counter. Instead, I received a courteous welcome to a small office, a firm hand shake from an immigration officer and impressive comments on my academic achievement.

By early August, I received Canada's "Landed Immigrant" offer. I was given a few months to confirm my acceptance by entering Canada. It sounded all too good to be true. Given the political situation, I wondered if Canada could change its decision at any time.

While I appreciated the offer, I was hesitant to leave the U.S. By then, I had looked up my final destination on folded paper maps. Ottawa, Capital of Canada, was a dot on a map, whose only attraction to my ignorant eyes was a few hour drive to two well known land marks: Niagara Falls and Montreal, the home of 1976 Olympics.

An American friend offered to drive me to Windsor, where I could take a flight to Ottawa. Mid-morning on August 24th, we drove into the Detroit-Windsor tunnel. The short drive under fast passing long neon lights felt never-ending until we exited the tunnel and arrived at the Canadian Customs. An officer approached our car as we were about to park. My friend explained the purpose of our trip. The officer asked me to get out the car and follow him to a small office.

"An Iranian," he said to another officer. I took that as a code for "Inadmissible".

"Welcome to Canada," said the other officer as he rose to shake my hand. "Please have a seat."

He asked a few questions, reviewed my papers and started filling a white-pink-yellow multi sheet form. My eyes were pinned to his fingers, as if I could prevent him from writing "Inadmissible".

"Almost done," he said when he finally passed me the form to sign. I signed.

He put aside a folder of information sheets. He then signed and stamped the form, separated some of the sheets and put them in his folder. He put the rest in the information folder and handed me the folder, shook my hand and wished me a safe trip to Ottawa.

In that precious folder, there was a yellow sheet, one I used to call my Yellow Canadian Green Card. It was not merely a work permit. It was a life-long privilege to live and work anywhere in Canada. I cherished it.

I arrived in Ottawa on a sunny afternoon. A friend picked me up from the airport and drove me to downtown on his way to work. On our way, we drove on a road that went through a farm, then along a winding canal. I felt as if travelling through a post-card scene.

My friend dropped me off on Albert Street. Seeing many flocks of office workers, screeching buses and small cars making their way through the narrow streets, I figured the Ottawa dot was not as small as I had once perceived.

I applied for my health card at the OHIP office and walked to the OC Transpo office, then on Slater Street, where I got an $18.00 monthly bus pass. I walked back to Confederation Square where I indulged in watching boats going through the locks from the Rideau Canal to Ottawa River. I finally sat in a Spark Street café, reflecting. This beautiful city with its old buildings, charismatic downtown core and well-dressed office crowds was no longer a lifeless dot on a map but a connection to Europe. I liked it.

But soon came the winter. First the snow, then a cold Thanksgiving in October. In November, more snow. Then a brutally cold and icy Christmas, then more snow. On the first day of spring, I celebrated the Iranian New Year staring at a mountain of snow, feeling regretful for moving so close to the North Pole.

It was almost April when I pulled out my Yellow Canadian Green Card from my safety deposit box. With no spring in sight I decided to spend the Easter holidays with friends in Michigan. I needed a visa. Given the broken political ties between Iran and the U.S., I expected nothing but rejection. Nonetheless, I took my Iranian passport and my yellow paper and headed to the US embassy—then on Elgin Street.

To my surprise, without being questioned extensively, I got a one-year multiple entry visitor visas. My Yellow Canadian Green Card had apparently given me a prominent identity that was difficult to acquire with my Iranian passport at that time. This new identity gave me confidence and a sense of belonging that was yet too early for me to recognize.

A few weeks later, at the Detroit airport, I walked to an immigration officer who shouted, “Next!”

“The purpose of your trip?” he asked.

“Visiting my friends,” I said.

He showed not much interest in my answer. Instead, took his time paging through my Iranian passport and browsing my yellow paper.

I was waiting for him to ask how long I was to stay in the U.S.

Instead, he caught me off guard. “When will you return home?”

“Home?” I asked.

“Ottawa, of course!” He said.

Not until then, I had considered Ottawa my home. Ottawa, with its brutal winter, had been a rather temporary stop until the hostage crisis was over.

My Easter U.S. visit fell short of all pleasures. The weather was brittle cold and windy. Most friends were gone home for the holidays. Those who stayed on campus were busy. As if I had not had my fair share of disappointment, a snow storm closed the Ottawa airport and the flight back to Ottawa was rerouted to Montreal. On the bus from Montreal, I first cursed Ottawa for its brutal weather then myself for my cowardliness. “I should have stayed in the U.S. illegally.” I thought. But soon I recalled the prominent status my yellow paper had given me. I decided to accept Ottawa’s temperamental weather. “I will learn to skate.” I vowed.

I continued to travel with my Iranian passport and my yellow paper, until I became a Canadian citizen and got my Canadian passport in 1984. With a Canadian Passport I no longer required visa to travel the world—well almost anywhere with a few exceptions.

My Yellow Canadian Green Card sat dormant in a safety deposit box until 1991 when I went for a visit to Iran. On that trip, I did not take my Canadian passport. I went to Iran with my Iranian passport, my yellow paper, and a handful of cards that were forgotten to be removed from my purse before leaving Ottawa.

On the way back from Iran, I was almost barred from boarding my connecting flight at Dubai and Sophia airports. My Yellow Canadian Green Card was accused of being a copy and not an original document.

"It should be white. Why is it yellow?" Flight check-in officers asked. "It is a copy." He pointed to a small footnote on my yellow paper.

Copy or not, that yellow paper was genuine. I was a Canadian citizen and no check-in officer could have barred me from returning home—to Canada. I covered the check-in counter with anything that showed my Canadian affiliation: drivers license, health card, numerous credit cards, and a handful of Canadian tire money bills.

"If you don't believe me, call the Canadian consulate." I told the officers. My confident tone worked. Armed officers who had approached me backed off. I was let to board the plane.

At the Ottawa airport, I was prepared.

"Next!" A Customs Canada officer called.

I marched to him, holding tight to my yellow paper and my Iranian passport in one hand and my deck of cards in the other.

"Where is the original?" He asked.

I had no answer. I did not know.

"I am a Canadian citizen. My passport is in the safety deposit box," I gave him the bank address and babbled an account of my life in Ottawa—bike rides along the canal, Sunday brunches in Byward Market, skiing and snowshoeing in Gatineau hills, warming up by wood stoves in ski huts, the Winterlude . . .

He interrupted me. "Who is the Prime Minister of Canada?"

"Mr. Mulroney," I said. But soon a shadow of doubt fell upon me. I had been away for three weeks.

"He was when I left, I said, feeling guilty. "I had not kept up with the news," I said.

"He still is." He stamped my passport, "Please get a certified copy for your next trip."

He smiled and handed me my yellow paper. "Welcome home," he said.

When Kansas Met Kanook

by Nedra Nash

I was a resident, until third grade, in a Missouri state park which my Dad built for the U.S. National Park Service and then educated through to Grade 12 in the arid landscape and culture of Kansas City, Kansas. I longed inside for the historically elegant architecture and culture revealed in parts of Kansas City, Missouri. My college freshman summer found me working Mother Hubbard's Cupboard at Santa's Workshop, White Face Mountain, N.Y. In 1957, the Canadian dollar was worth six cents more than the U.S., and therefore a strong inducement for a French Canadian Naval recruiting Lieutenant to spend weekends drinking in the pub we college kids retired to after work. One night, after exercise 'round a pool table somewhere, he offered me a ride home in his racing green, M.G. convertible. I have no idea what attracted him to me; his car and his attention attracted me to him.

Over the summer, this tall, bear-hug-chummy gentleman, stubby of nose, bright, witty, partnered my first adult romance. Our 12 year age difference seemed as naught to me. Perhaps I appeared as "renewal, refreshment" in his weekend "healing regime" from a deep, hurtful, serious romance: his first.

He could stand by the bar for three hours, never tell the same story twice, keep all around totally amused and sing risqué Naval songs as well. I learned to nurse one rum and coke for at least an hour. I admired his eclectic knowledge sourced from a wide ranging mind that fed on long hours alone, recruiting through the villages of Québec, a mind originally trained by a classical college education such as the Montréal male elite finished at age 17. He was supposed to become a lawyer; he certainly had the mind for it. He ran away, however, after graduation and joined the Navy in 1943. He saw service against U-boats, and learned English from comic books. With the English proficiency came the Lieutenancy.

That Christmas he came to Kansas hoping my Mum would allow me to ride back to college in New York State with him. She didn't.

The next summer my college offered a job touring farms in Saskatchewan on an Anglican Mission van, with free train travel out and back. I took it. He proposed before I left. I knew my mum would kill me *if* I didn't finish college. I told him we'd talk about it when I returned. I returned. He didn't meet me.

Fall 1958 was a great empty desert inside, a time for black "scanties" and feelings of confusion! That Christmas, however, Mum came East. She, my sister and I visited Montreal!

Veni, vidi, vincit: I came, I saw, *it* conquered! Here was my city with "panache", an artful mix of European architecture, culture, chic *and* it spoke French! (Maybe not to me but, if I worked hard with my five college credits of Parisian proficient French, *I* might speak to it!)

It took three years, but slowly, after college and a six-month work stint in cold, penurious New York City, I ventured north again, waitressed at White Face, met the world bobsled teams in various languages and the spring of '61 found myself a secretary at Plattsburgh TV, 30 miles south of Montreal. Working my way through two jobs between March and June 30th, (being fired from the last), suddenly I felt free! Free to go where inner desire had me slowly vectored: *la belle ville historique de Montréal!*

In Montréal, I used an employment agency to find secretarial work! Subtext? Maybe someday I'd run into HIM but . . . for now?

What a great place just to live!

I had to get to an interview with *The Montreal Star* as secretary to the Art Director (perfect!). I sought, for at least a half an hour in Old Montreal for "St James Street". All I saw was St. Jacques! (So much for college French!). As interview time drew really near, it dawned on me, French city, French names!

I got the job. Three years passed with 9 to 5 for hours, then night work in theatre for fun. At 26, the need for more dollars for a better future bludgeoned my psyche. Armed with my Arts Baccalaureate and Québec's Protestant School System's need for more teachers, I got a job in Arvida, Québec, teaching Grade 9 and 10 English. There, where peonies drip heavy bonnets of wet snow to the end of September, I taught school for the first time in my life *and* met a young electrical engineer . . . from Australia!

But that's another story! Suffice to say, the rest of our lives brought residences as west as Kitimat, B.C. including a new babe, east as far as Kingston, Ontario, with a new babe from Viet Nam. The next 10 years were divided between Hong Kong, Tokyo, Japan and Sydney, Australia. There, faced with a family crisis, it was my choice to return to the country where I knew I could always make a living and a home, Canada.

Ottawa, Ontario, 1987, was new to us but was only a gentle distance from my source, Montreal. It comforted with close, rural surroundings, rolling scenery recalling the Missouri park and the farms of Kansas, enriched with its Franco-Ontarian culture and federal government intrigue, Ottawa, with its proximity to old friends from Kingston and Montreal, sustained and nurtured this fortunate transplant and family in that challenging transition so oft given those in their late forties.

"Transplant"? Nay! Surely "Hybrid" now!

Prairie Pioneers – Triumphs and Tragedies

by Sylvia Findlay

Poverty stricken, seduced by promises of a better life, four sets of my great-grandparents and their families emigrated from Western Ukraine to Canada in the spring of 1899.

This is the story of two of these families, my paternal great-grandparents, Kindrat and Teklia, and my maternal great-grandparents, Hrynko and Teklia.

A large contingent of Ukrainian pioneers travelled together to settle in Manitoba. Most were strangers until they met on their two-month journey. The first leg of the trip was by train to Hamburg where they boarded the ship SS Palatia, travelling by steerage to Montreal. The next leg was by train to Winnipeg where they were met by government officials and driven by horse and wagon to Shoal Lake, a distance of two hundred miles. Having left a continental, temperate climate they were horrified, upon their arrival, to find themselves in a Manitoba May snowstorm. Living in tents, exhausted and chilled the immigrants had no resistance to scarlet fever. Thirty-eight children and three adults died a few days after their arrival.

My paternal great-grandparents, Kindrat, 52 years, and Teklia, 44 years, a daughter, son-in-law, a grandson and three sons, my grandfather, Peter, the eldest of the boys, were in the community of immigrants who arrived in Canada in May of 1899. The five-year-old grandson perished in the scarlet fever epidemic.

A homestead was established but my great-grandfather, Kindrat, a carpenter, succumbed to cancer in January of 1902. Twelve days later a grandson was born to Peter and his wife Michelina in a sod hut on a rainy January day. Despite her grief at losing her beloved husband, Teklia, a competent midwife, delivered Peter's child. This babe was my father Joseph.

Life was difficult and widows and widowers remarried. Teklia's new partner was a fine man who had suffered terribly since his arrival in Canada. He had lost all five of his little daughters to the scarlet fever epidemic and a few years later his wife died due to a tragic accident. Grief stricken he was unable to establish his homestead in the designated time, therefore it was repossessed by the government.

My paternal great-grandmother was married to her partner, Mike, for 38 years. He lived to the age of ninety seven passing away in 1941 and she lived to ninety, passing away in 1944.

I remember my great-grandmother and my step great-grandfather. I recall they lived in a tiny overheated house with a steep staircase and they treated us numerous great-grandchildren to hard raspberry-shaped candies.

My father and his grandmother, Teklia, shared a strong bond. She doted on the child, pampering him, singing songs and telling him stories about life in Ukraine. He shared these vivid stories with his children, making Ukraine very real to us. In 1990, I visited the village Teklia had called home. It was just as my Dad had described it; not much had changed.

My maternal great-grandparents were also members of the community who arrived in Canada in May of 1899. Hrynko, 44 years and Teklia, 37 years, arrived with a family consisting of a son, Michael my grandfather, and five daughters. The two youngest girls perished in the scarlet fever epidemic.

The pioneers were grief stricken by the severe losses they had suffered. My grandfather Michael, a boy of fourteen at the time, was called on to help with the burials. He dug shallow graves for his little sisters.

Despite this tragedy the family worked hard to settle their homestead of rocks, clay and poplar. Hard work and perseverance paid off but the cash flow was nil. Michael at fourteen, walked forty miles to find employment with well established families who had arrived decades before the Ukrainian settlers. A bright lad, his employers helped and encouraged him to become fluent in English.

A cherished baby daughter was born to Hrynko and Teklia in 1901, However, in July of 1903 tragedy struck again. Teklia and her three little daughters were killed by lightning. The family now consisted of Michael, his sister Anastasia and father Hrynko. Two years later in 1905 when Michael was twenty, Hrynko fell into an open well: unable to climb out of the pit he died of exposure. A family of eight had arrived in 1899 and was diminished to only two by 1905.

Michael married Marinka; a dark-eyed, good natured girl. They raised several children, my mother Frances, the eldest, was born in 1907.

Life was not easy for Michael and Marinka. Michael was more of a dreamer than a farmer. He loved politics, public speaking and inventing things. His attempts at securing patents were unsuccessful.

I remember him as a happy entertaining grandfather who loved spending time with his multitude of grandchildren. He helped us put on concerts to entertain our parents. He grew raspberries, crab-apples and kept bees, a pastime which was exotic to me.

Wed for sixty-seven years, Michael was predeceased by Marinka in 1973, aged 84. He lived to 94 years of age and died in 1979.

I knew my grandparents very well and have happy memories of staying with them as a child so I could attend catechism.

Our family is eternally grateful to these far seeing ancestors who made great sacrifices to ensure their descendants would have a better quality of life. Thank you.

Settling Down

by Bobby Salvin

My stepfather drove me, our sons Alan, almost four, and Ian, one-and-a-half, to Liverpool docks with my mother, stepsister Kathleen and my cousin, Mary. They all stayed to wave us goodbye. It was a sad moment. We didn't know if or when we would see each other again. We waved until we could no longer see them, then turning, I dried my eyes and we went to our cabin. It was 1957, and we were on our way to Canada to join my husband, Jim.

I treated the voyage as a holiday. It was great. I was able to devote time to the children during the day and in the evening, there was a steward to watch over them whilst I was entertained elsewhere on the ship. I played bingo, saw movies and watched live shows.

At one point the ship had to change course because there was a huge iceberg on our route. The boys and I went on deck and could see it looming on the horizon, so white in the sunshine. Then, the weather changed. The seas were tremendous. I revelled in it and was disappointed that I wasn't allowed on deck.

There were noticeably fewer people in the dining room for a few days. It didn't seem long before we were travelling up the St. Lawrence Seaway, past Quebec City and the Jacques-Cartier Bridge. We had to fill in all kinds of forms and were given our "landed immigrant" papers.

At last, we reached Montreal on August 27th. After the official red tape had been dealt with, we landed and were finally reunited with Jim.

It was so good to be together, even if it was in another country. The children were a little shy at first, but it soon wore off. We were bundled into a taxi and were off to the station for the ride to Ottawa.

When we left the dock and turned onto the street, I was terrified. We were hurtling along on the wrong side of the road! Jim took my hand and reminded me that in Canada, we drove on the right side of the road. That calmed me a bit, but it still felt so strange to me.

After the train ride to Ottawa, we took a taxi to our new home on Bell Street. It was the top floor of a large renovated family house. We had two bedrooms, a large eat-in ktchen, living room, bathroom and spacious hall to connect them all. I was delighted to find the furniture in place when we entered. The house was close to Dows Lake Park and it was a wonderful place for the children. They enjoyed playing under the big old trees and walking beside the lake.

I found the heat almost unbearable. I had never experienced such hot weather so I enjoyed the park as much as the boys. At times in the house I felt the heat so much that I would open the fridge and stick my head into it for a breath of cooler air, but I was with Jim and our two sons, so I was content.

We soon used up some of the supplies Jim had provided for us, so I set out for the corner store with the boys. It was part way down the street and a pleasant walk for all. I was pleased to find it was similar to the local shops in England and so went to the counter and waited for the clerk.

"Can I help you?" he asked.

"Thank you. I'd like four pints of milk, please."

He looked at me strangely. "Wouldn't it be better to take two quarts?" he asked. I was started. I was used to the milkman leaving four pint bottles on the step every day. Confused, I agreed with him. He bagged the milk and I toted the two cartons home wondering how many more such instances I was to meet. Later, I even began to write an English/Canadian dictionary.

Pavements were sidewalks

Shops were stores

Loaves were bread

Trams were streetcars, etc.

The boys and I explored the neighbourhood on foot. I had them both wearing child harnesses whenever we went for a walk, as it was easier to keep them safe, especially two active toddlers in a strange environment. One day, a woman stopped me. "It's disgusting to have your children tied up like animals," she declared.

"At least they're safe," I said, crossly. She snorted and continued on her way. I couldn't help being astonished at being accosted in such a way by a stranger.

That spring, I became dreadfully homesick. I longed for the balmy spring air of England, the violets in the hedgerows and the primroses in the woods. I lost weight to the point that my doctor suggested a tonic and, I couldn't believe it, a pint of porter a day! Jim was most happy to get it for me and made sure that I drank it regularly.

We acquired a puppy and called her Pal. She was part collie and part German Shepard. She was wonderful with the boys and they enjoyed romping together, both indoors and at the park. She became a real guard dog for them. If someone came anywhere near, she would walk between them and the boys. If they tried to get closer, she began to growl. It must have been instinct because we didn't train her that way.

In August, we bought a car. We were all very excited about it. We had been getting about by bus and streetcar and that had limited the scope of our travels. I was delighted with the ease with which we were able to get the car. We obtained a loan from the bank and the car was ours.

We soon began to explore the surrounding countryside. One Sunday, we drove into the province of Quebec, feeling very daring, and visited Wakefield. By that time the fall leaves had all gone but it was still a very pretty drive. We were starting to feel settled; we now had a dog and a car. What more could any family need?

And So Life Went On

by Douglas Thomas Shaw

I was born in Liverpool England on the 24th day of July in 1919. At the time my father was in the Canadian army stationed in Seaford, England. He was a sergeant for The Royal Canadian Artillery and his major duty included setting up drafts to go to France. One day he included his own name in the draft, but the colonel spotted it and that was the end of his adventure. When the draft was assembled it was paraded to the railway station with a band playing Colonel Bogey March (Bridge on the River Kwai). My mother always hated that tune because very often the boys being paraded never came back.

In Canada, my father must have been good at his job for the Montreal Light, Heat and Power Company, which I vaguely remember. We lived in the east end of Maisonneuve, Montreal for three or four years. Mother was very homesick being so far away from her sisters and the rest of her family so we decided that we were to move back to England to check things out. We boarded the boat for Liverpool that spring. Unfortunately, things were slow in England and the decision was made to come back to Montreal. We left Liverpool in June of 1924 and upon our arrival, Dad found a house for us on Boyer St. About this time, Dad was hired back with the same company, only this time building a Hydro Electric Plant in Cedars, just west of Vaudreuil.

This was a great place for a small boy to grow up because the fields were full of old construction machines like dump trucks, railway tracks, etc. Thankfully, I got to meet other boys in my neighborhood. My friends at this time included Albert Holdway, his sister Rosie,

Tommy Higgins, his sister Katherine, Vic Hayter, and Tommy Auburn (Later to be known as Magic Tom). Magic Tom was always doing magic tricks even back then in 1924. Sadly, his father died a couple of years previous to this because the Spanish flu was prevalent in those days. His uncle was Mr. Pruner, so half the time he was called Tom Pruner although his last name was Auburn.

I lost track of Tom until I started school in Montreal, when we bumped into each other once more. The next time I can remember us meeting was while I was in the army stationed in Brockville. He was doing a magic show there. Another fellow that I met on and off as time went on was Bill Grant, also from Cedars. He was in the RCAF during the war as an aeronautical engineer. The other fellows that I mentioned, I never saw again.

The next big event—and I mean big event—in the Shaw household was the birth of my sister Joyce on the 27th of October 1927. I said it was a big event and it was, because it was the first girl that came into the family and the first live birth my mother had apart from me. She said she had two sons before Joyce, but they only lived a few hours due to a problem with their blood. The doctor officiating was Dr. Clement who was assisted by Mrs. Chevrier, who I think was a sort of local midwife. Anyway, Joyce was born without any complications. There was more noise and commotion followed by wailing which I guess was Joyce announcing her arrival. A short time later, Mrs. Chevrier brought the baby to meet me. My recollection of this was that she sure was noisy for one so small.

Needless to say, our lives changed appreciably from here on. I found it interesting to see how my sister developed. Miss Hayter, a relative of Vic Hayter, came and stayed with us to keep the house running okay. Joyce was christened in about February of 1927 in

Coteau Junction, that was the closest Anglican Church. I think she was supposed to be named Marion after mother but I remember Mrs. Holdway suggested on the way to the church that she be christened Joyce Marion Shaw instead. As it would turn out, three of mother's sisters recently had had daughters who were all named Joyce after my sister Joyce was born.

That summer, we went back to the U.K. It was exciting for me to see my cousins again and also to go to the beach at New Brighton. During our stay at Liverpool, we lived with my mother's sister, Auntie Maggie. At that time, my cousin George Dunn lived next door so there was always a lot going on. I remember Christmas that year, although I have forgotten what I got for Christmas I do remember that it was wrapped in blue tissue paper. I was enrolled in Sunday School and the teacher had this idea that I would be able to tell them all about living on a Canadian farm on the prairies. Little did she know!

Anyhow, we returned to Canada in about June of 1929. When we left Liverpool, I remember that my Auntie Katie gave me a Meccano set that thrilled me to bits. We had to take the train from St. John's to Montreal. I remember that we traveled in immigrant cars with wooden seats. Dad met us in Montreal. I think that we stayed with the Adams on Boyer Street. Dad went off to Cedars to get the house fixed up for us. It was located on the bank of the Headrace.

Shortly after it was time to start school. I was in Grade One all by myself. My teachers name was Miss GodMeyer, who did not know much about teaching. As a matter of fact, my dad took it upon himself to check her credentials with the Department of Education in Quebec. They came back with the information that she never even finished High School, let alone Teachers College. So Mr. McBurney, the head of the English section of the department in Quebec, volunteered to suggest a person who would fulfill the requirements. She was a Miss Ross, who turned out to be a top-notch teacher, and had several years of experience with the Grenfell Group in Labrador.

Miss Ross turned out to be a cracker jack. Often she took us for hikes in the fields that I found most interesting and I still remember some of the things she pointed out to us. Unfortunately, Miss Ross left at the end of the term which was too bad; I guess that the school was too small for her. The next teacher we got was Mrs. Pye from Ottawa, who had a lot of experience and she turned out to be a very good teacher. She was the aunt of Lester Patrick, who was the manager of the NHL hockey team in New York.

The next teacher we had was just a girl out of MacDonald College. She came from a farm family in Lachute. I thought that she was a pretty good teacher, although some of the older fellows gave her a hard time because she was so young. I remember that they used to bring bits of junk that they had found, telling her that it fell off of a car similar to hers. I guess she liked me because one day she invited me to go with her to her farm in Lachute. One other stunt we pulled on her was one day we caught a mouse, which was tied by its tail to the clapper of the bell on her desk. Needless to say, she screamed the first time she picked it up.

Well, time went on and we eventually left Cedars and moved back to Montreal, this time to a house on Christopher Columbus St.

It was time to meet Elma Graham. One afternoon, I went with Mike Polard to our usual place to catch the #80 street car up north. It was the 30th of October and it was the day of the commencement party of the previous class. Our class was invited to go to the party to find out what it was all about, and well, we would be going through the same thing next year. On my streetcar there were a number of

Grade 11 girls, including Elma. This was very convenient because before we got off the car at Park Ave, we were chatting like old friends. Little did I know that I had been talking to my future girlfriend who would eventually become my wife. So that is how that happened.

In no time at all we were meeting on the streetcar and other places from then on. This livened things up considerably because she was the first girl that I met in High School. I forgot to mention that our school was completely segregated as far as gender was concerned but what the heck, it worked out just fine. Well I eventually married her, didn't I? Before long we were meeting every day either going to or from school.

Well that takes up to about the end of June 1942, the year I graduated from McGill for engineering. As I remember the graduation ceremony, it was held outside on the campus. The weather was semi nice with sunshine half the time. From what I remember, it seemed that most of the grads were in uniform. People attending were my father and mother, sister Joyce and of course Elma. Incidentally, I realized too late that at that time we should have made arrangements for Joyce to go to McGill, but no one thought about it at the time, so it was an opportunity lost. There was a graduation ball that night but I couldn't go because I had to be back in Brockville the next morning, so we settled for a horse and buggy ride instead. Anyways I caught the eleven o'clock train back to Brockville and got back on time. So all's well that ends well.

And so, life went on . . .

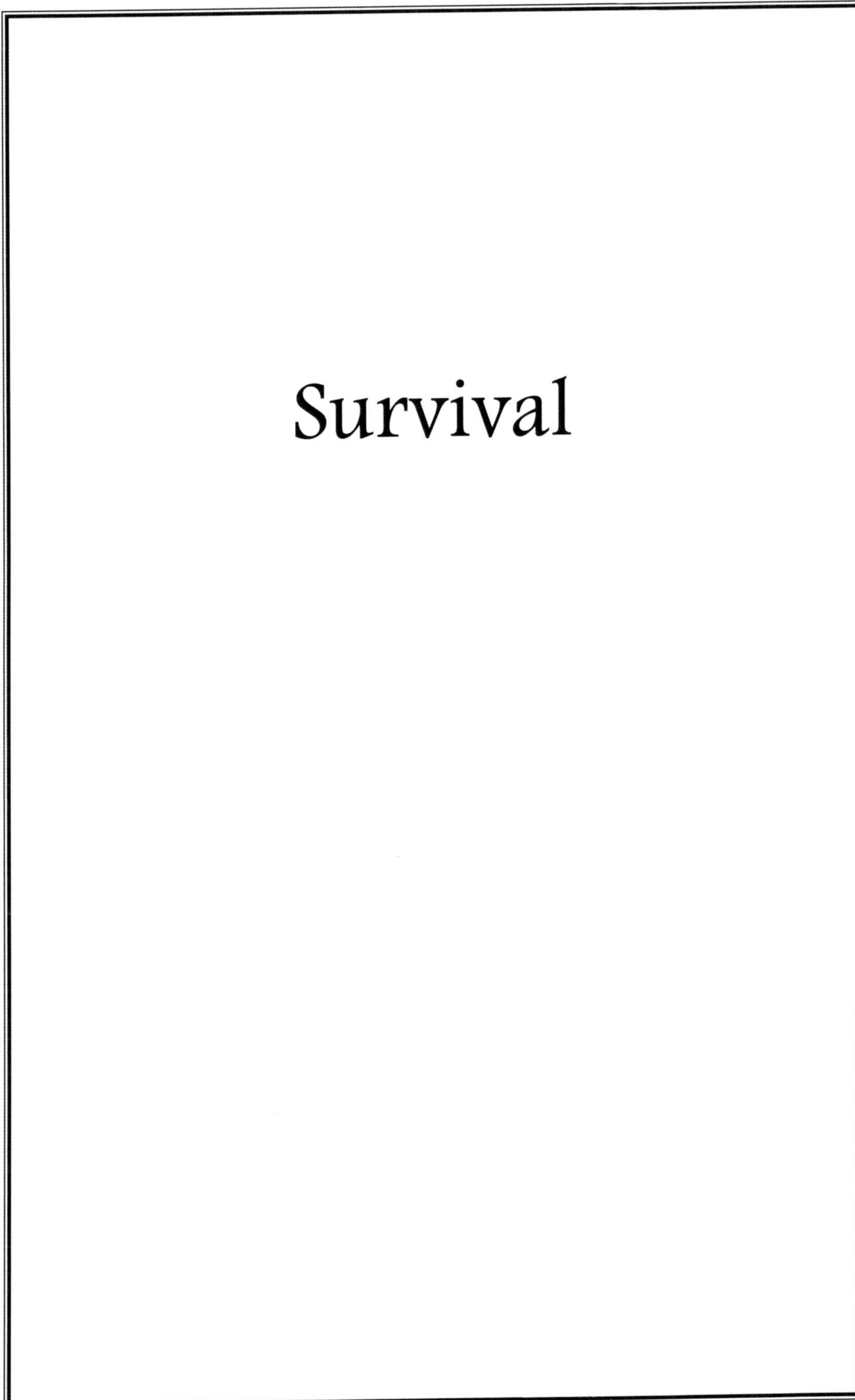

Survival

A Dramatic End to a Perfect Day

by Ruth Knapp

As he rounded the corner, Jeff stared in horror at the sight before him. There, at the side of the road were firemen vehemently hosing down Ozzie's motor home. Ozzie and his family had been enjoying the weekend with Jeff's family at Constance Bay, about thirty kilometers North West of Ottawa, Ontario. Since Jeff knew his dad, Bob, had to go to work early, he knew Ozzie would be bringing his mom, Ruth, and his sister, Wendy, home about this time. He could see the beast of a vehicle lying nose down in a fourteen-foot ditch, stopped only by a large tree. Jeff's heart throbbed in his chest. His breath came in short gulps. Where were his mom, his sister and their friends?

The jovial groups were returning home from a fun-packed weekend at the cottage. Fortunately, they were not speeding. On one of the major roadways, not three miles from home, Ozzie tried to turn the wheel slightly to avoid a bump. The wheel did not respond. In fact, the steering wheel spun around in his hand; the tie-rod had snapped! The RV immediately began to follow the slant of the road. The ditch was inevitable. Ozzie tapped the brakes ever so gently and prayed that the vehicle would not roll.

He began issuing curt orders. "We're going in!" he shouted. Brace yourselves. Cover your heads" That's all the time he had before our world went topsy-turvy.

Ozzie, himself, flew out the left front window where the windshield had been only seconds before. He landed on top of it head first. As he pulled himself up, the blood ran profusely, and painfully, from his bald head, down his face, covering his hands completely. Paramount in his mind was the safety of his passengers coupled with the fear of explosion from the volatile propane on board. Immediate evacuation was essential. Glancing over his shoulder, he saw that Wendy had landed on her back beside him but she seemed to be unharmed as she headed up the embankment to flag down someone to help.

The female passengers, sitting in the dining area of the motor home, had been thrown around like popcorn in a popper. Ozzie's wife, Gwen, flew across the aisle and banged her shoulder, first into the stove, then into the sink. Ozzie and Gwen's two daughters were thrown into the front window which shattered, but did not move. Their faces were sprinkled with glass shards. The other passenger, Jeff's mom, was flipped into the air, somersaulted onto the ceiling, landing roughly wrapped around the base of the drivers' seat. She was pinned between the steering wheel, a cupboard door and the table top which had split in half. All of these things and more were piled on top of her. Lying pinned frightened and watching the scenario, involved, yet somehow removed, Ruth also anticipated an explosion. She was sure, being the only one pinned down, and watching everyone else leave the RV on Ozzie's command, that she would be the only fatality.

However, much to her relief, Ozzie, with no thought for his own safety, jumped back into the RV and little by little was able to free her. As she looked around she realized what devastation had taken place in the space of three seconds. All the cupboards were ripped from the walls, the stove and refrigerator torn from their mountings were left with their doors gaping ajar, hanging loosely on lone hinges. The cupboard had spewed their contents all over the passengers as well as the vehicle.

The passenger who graphically registered the contents of the cupboard was Ruth's little, white toy poodle, Missy. She was totally covered with butter and coffee grounds. It was as though she had been dipped in "Shake n' bake". Her little body was quivering forlornly in the stairwell. She had been forgotten in the confusion, a most unusual, pathetic sight!

Within minutes the ambulance arrived. In reality the ride to the Queensway-Carleton Hospital was not very long but to the victims it seemed interminable and dream-like. Nothing about the event seemed quite real.

Jeff arrived in the hospital, face ashen, hands perspiring, unsure of what he would find. To his great relief, as he walked through the door, he saw his mother clutching her buttered poodle while she was phoning him to come and rescue the poor little thing. His mom was alive and mobile. Jeff learned that all the other passengers were safe and only suffering from minor injuries. His relief was immeasurable, though short-lived, as he realized he had to take this greasy, coffee-covered poodle home and bathe her instead of going to visit his girlfriend as he had planned.

Driving home, Jeff and Missy passed the scene of the accident again. The firemen were gone and there was Ozzie's home-on-wheels a mass of mangled metal, crumpled aluminium and broken glass. How lucky, he felt, that his family and friends had survived.

If it Could Happen to Me

by Patricia Stockwell

Seventeen years ago in November of 1992, I was wandering the streets of London, Ontario, Canada in shorts and bare feet, the temperature only eight degrees Celsius. I was swearing out loud. Little people were arguing in my head. "You're crazy." "No, I am not." I yelled at them "Just shut up, all of you." Passersby stared at me, taking a wide berth around me.

I was suffering from a psychotic episode brought on by recovered memories of childhood sexual abuse. Two weeks before, I had gone to a weekend retreat centered around 'mat' trips where the goal was release of frozen emotional pain. I was blindfolded and put into a semi-hypnotic state through the use of Traeger body work. My body began moving of its own accord. I crawled and rolled across the mattress, all the while believing that I was being assaulted.

That night, after we had all gone to bed, I felt intense heat surge down the middle of my head, like electrical charges firing across the center of my brain. The scorching heat spread down my right arm into my hand. My fingers began to clench and unclench like a wild animal scratching at a cage. I think my brain chemistry was dramatically altered that night and those chemical changes unlocked a trap door to long-buried memories of childhood abuse.

When I returned home, I suffered from anxiety attacks and more body memories—my body would jerk and twist and turn into contortions, all without my conscious control. Then, once the gyrations subsided, old frozen sadness and anger would surface.

About this time, I started to believe that I was a witch and my friends and I were part of a coven. Together, we were fighting evil in the world. One night, I lit candles to summon the good spirits; then, I systematically burned my collection of African masks, convinced that they were infused with evil energy. I was hot so I stripped down to my underwear, turned the music up full blast and danced half-naked in the backyard, pretending to gather huge balls of energy in the air and toss them over the roof top to witches on the other side of the world.

These delusions went on for a good two weeks until one night, I decided to take a hot bath to calm down. As I watched the water lap around my toes, I imagined that I was in an ocean of polluted water. The earth was dying and the polluted water was flooding the earth. I was drowning in the polluted water. Suddenly, I began to shake uncontrollably. I bolted upright and grabbed the black bathmat lying beside the tub and wrapped it around my shoulders. The black dye began to bleed into the tub. More pollution! Germs! Viruses! We were all going to die!. In a panic, I rolled onto the floor beside the bath tub. I am not sure how long I lay there, cold and terrified but in the cold light of the morning, I realized how much trouble I was in so I phoned a friend. That friend took me to St. Joseph's Hospital where they admitted me to the psychiatric floor and administered anti-psychotic drugs.

I am one of the lucky ones. I survived this incident. I count my blessings every night that I am not still wandering the streets, arguing with the voices in my head. At the time of the psychosis, I was a mother of teenage daughters and a professional teacher. Now, I am retired and a grandmother. To-day, I enjoy excellent mental health but I always think, "If it could happen to me, it could happen to anyone".

Fears and Phobias

by Linda Wilson

As a child I was lucky—secure in the safe circle of my family and happy with the way my life was unfolding. I never had cause to be frightened, beyond the normal childhood wariness of strangers and the other dangerous things most parents warned their children about. If the truth is told, my biggest fear was probably that my parents would find out whenever I did something deemed "bad". Now that was worthy of fear!

Early on, however, I did learn that some people are fearful of things the rest of us are not. My father's brother Aubrey, who was just about the most interesting person we children knew, was one of these people. In keeping with this status, he had not one phobia but two.

The first was a terrible fear of thunder storms. In the summer we often had what were referred to as heat storms, and there would be lightening flashing across the sky like a veritable fireworks show, but with no rain or even thunder. There was a huge stand of lilacs just outside the porch at Grammie Kirk's farm on the Florida Road. It was the perfect place in which to stand while the storm raced across the sky, and when the rain came down, it was thick enough to keep you warm and dry.

Poor Uncle Aubrey, however, would be in the house, pacing the floor, becoming more and more anxious, until finally he would grab his keys and literally run for his truck, where he would hunker down until the storm was over. Every one knew how terrified he was, but I never heard it discussed or even commented upon. In a family of very opinionated and often critical people,(they were Scots Presbyterians after all) it is interesting to note that while he would have been criticized for buying the wrong make of truck, or spending too much money frivolously, there was no mention of this embarrassing quirk in his personality.

Being children, and therefore self-centered little beasts, my cousins, brothers and I were not above exploiting a person's weakness. Aubrey loved to work, and he was busy from dawn to dusk. The only thing he liked more than working, was putting us children to work. We were convinced that he laid awake nights thinking of jobs for us to do while he was away all day at his job at the Tatamagouche Creamery. We would have to thin the turnips as they came up, or pick potato bugs off the young plants and put them in a glass jar, so he could dispose of them later. That was our least favourite task.

Sometimes he wanted us to pick up rocks in the pasture, and throw them up onto the stone fence that divided the fields. The stone fence was a marvelous thing. It was about 6 or 8 feet across and maybe 4 feet high and it stretched for what seemed like miles. There were huge stones and smaller ones, all settled together, with grass and blueberry plants and even a few wild raspberry bushes growing along in places. It had been there forever, and over time had become a refuge for small creatures, sheltering them from the deep snow in winter, and the heat of the sun in summer.

On lovely summer afternoons we often found garter snakes there, curled up and sleeping in the sun. This was our big opportunity for some fun. Uncle Aubrey hated snakes. It was a big joke to us kids, and we would catch the biggest one we could find, and put it in a bucket, and take it up to the yard. When Uncle Aubrey was finished the evening milking, someone would call him over to see what had been found, and then throw the dazed creature up in the air. Poor Aubrey would shriek and run for the house. We found this hilarious! We were never punished for this rotten behavior, although our other transgressions were quickly dealt with. I believe now, that Aubrey was probably self-conscious about his irrational fear, and didn't want to call attention to himself in this way. Uncle Aubrey, if you are up there listening . . . I'm sorry.

Lessons From My Mother

by Sherman Chow

Sometime in 1947, we became car owners. By then, two years after the war, new cars were finally available and gas rationing in Canada was only an unpleasant memory. My father, who had acquired a driving permit, took delivery of our first car, a new Buick. It was then that we discovered Dad was not a good driver. To be fair, in those days, driving required considerable amounts of manual dexterity and practice because our car, like most of the others of the period, had no automatic transmission, power breaks, or power steering. Dad, having had no car, did not have a chance to learn to drive. Moreover, he had the unfortunate propensity to get drowsy behind the wheel, especially after a substantial meal.

It was then that my mother decided to learn to drive and relieve some of the driving duties, especially when Dad felt tired. She could also use the car to visit friends and shop when Dad was at work. In those days there were no driving schools; the student, after acquiring a learner's permit, learned from someone who did not have any qualifications other than to be in possession of a valid driver's license.

My mother's first lessons took place on the deserted roads within the confines of the Experimental Farm in Ottawa where, after several false starts, she was able to get the car underway from a dead stop without stalling. Mother was not a tall woman; in order for her to reach the peddles, the seat had to be pushed forward leaving my mother straining to see over the steering wheel with it held almost against her chest.

After many hours in the Experimental Farm, mother managed to learn to steer and shift gears without lurching or grinding the gear box. Leaving the deserted streets of the Farm behind, the driving practice continued on the streets of the residential area where we lived. Parallel parking was difficult for her because the Buick was unusually heavy and it took considerable muscle power to turn the wheel. Nevertheless, she persisted and eventually became adept at reversing the Buick into tight parking spaces. Then they took to the country roads where my mother could gain experience in highway driving. Mother, like all novice drivers, dreaded the prospect of driving in downtown traffic. For that reason, she avoided the streets around the Chateau Laurier in her practice drives.

My mother being careful and thorough, delayed the Driver's Exam as long as possible, giving herself ample time to practice and memorize every regulation in the Driver's Handbook. Having done all she could, she was happy when she passed the Driver's Exam with flying colors the first time she tried. She dropped Dad off at a streetcar stop so that he could go back to the office, while she drove herself home.

Sitting in the driver's seat alone for the first time she was suddenly seized by panic; she wanted to leave the car parked until Dad got home from work. Then she realized that her fears were irrational, for she was now a licensed driver, legally permitted to drive anywhere she wished.

She decided that she must confront all of her fears, including driving in downtown traffic, for she knew that procrastination would only intensify it. Steeling herself, she started the car and drove on, not toward our house, but towards the Parliament Buildings. As she carefully maneuvered the Buick through the city traffic, fears slowly subsided, and she continued driving even as snow began to fall, not stopping until she was completely at ease alone behind the wheel.

When she finally pulled into our driveway, exhausted but triumphant, Dad had returned from work. Seeing Mother and the car were both missing, he feared the worst and was about to call the police.

Five years later, it was my mother who taught me to drive. More importantly, I learned by her example how to overcome fear.

Earthquake

by Bobby Salvin

A friend and I meet once a month for lunch, an event that we both enjoy. As she worked in a store in the Carlingwood Shopping Centre we met there on June the twenty-third. We were in a booth at the Family Restaurant when we became aware of a deep rumbling. There was a lot of construction in progress locally so we paid no attention. The rumbling increased until it seemed as if the world was filled with it. Everyone in the restaurant froze.

We looked at each other in consternation and at the same time we both grinned and said, "Earthquake!" We sat, holding onto the table as everything shook. It seemed to last forever but could only have been a few minutes and it then rumbled away. For a heartbeat there was utter silence then gradually people began to talk again.

It was amazing that there was no panic. People in the mall began to move toward the exits and the security guards were very much in evidence, watching as they left.

We finished our meal then my friend went back to work and I left for home. By then the mall was almost deserted. Store clerks stood in doorways chatting with each other as they watched the exodus.

I had things to do in Bells Corners so drove west on Carling to Moodie and then into Bells Corners. On the way I had to pull over as an ambulance screamed past and later on Moodie, again had to pull over for a fire engine. I finished my errands and turned from Richmond onto Baseline. As I passed bus stops I was surprised to see that they were crowded and traffic became very heavy and slow in both directions. I began to wonder what was happening but continued on my way home. At Centrepointe Drive the traffic was very congested. It took me twenty minutes to get from there to my home, usually less than a ten minute drive. The turn from Baseline onto Navaho at the lights was crazy. Cars were blocking the intersection in their haste to leave the city but fortunately the filter light allowed cars to exit Baseline.

As I opened the door on reaching home, the phone was ringing. My son in Kitchener was calling to check if all was well with me. There were messages from daughter, Lynn, in the Yukon and son, Alan, in downtown Ottawa also making sure that I was all right. I returned their calls and Alan had some interesting stories as to how people in his area had reacted to the earthquake.

Later, on checking through the house, the only thing I found amiss was one of my paintings had tilted slightly.

When I came to write this account I tried to remember how I felt during the earthquake. As I sat holding onto the table, my heart was racing and I felt slightly nauseated because the whole world seemed to be on the move. Perhaps that was because I was so frustrated knowing that there was absolutely nothing that I could do, other than stay put and ride it out. I admit that when it finally petered out I was mightily relieved.

Generosity Rubs Off

by Patricia Stockwell

When I was 59, I made a huge decision. I was totally stressed out with my job and I decided to retire early from teaching even though it meant that my pension would only be about $22,000 a year, before taxes. I sold my condo, broke even and moved to a one-bedroom apartment. Then, I made another big decision, to give up my car. I figured that alone would save me about $6,000 a year.

Once the retirement party was over and reality sank in, I became depressed about my financial situation. "How am I going to manage? I should have stayed in teaching until I was 65. I can't live on this skimpy amount of money!" Then, I got angry. "I've had it! I am not giving up everything. I am going to the Farmer's Market to buy myself some organic meat and vegetables and make myself a nice stew. I deserve to eat well!"

I managed to get on the right bus and get my provisions. I was waiting at the bus stop to go home when I spied another woman about my age with a shopping cart full of groceries. I moved next to her and started up a conversation, thinking maybe this was a woman in similar circumstances. "Have you been to the Farmer's Market?" I asked.

"No, I've just come from the food bank. I am feeding some extra mouths this month. I hate to rely on food banks but my nephew and his son are living with me for a while. My nephew, Bill, is out of work. I have custody of my grandson too. He's the same age as my nephew's boy so the house is lively these days."

I introduced myself as we boarded the same bus. "I'm Patty and I'm newly retired. To be honest, I am finding it quite an adjustment living on a pension."

"Tell me about it! Doreen's my name and I've been on welfare for over a year now. I hate it! I don't like being dependent on the Government. I am an independent woman. I like to be able to provide for myself and my own. I've been looking for a job as a waitress but everywhere that I apply, they say I am too old. Probably too slow! I am only 59! I am still healthy. I can work!"

"Well, you have a big heart, Doreen, taking in all those people on a welfare allowance," I sympathized.

"What else am I going to do? They're family. I don't have much but what I do have, I like to share. I just wish I could make nicer meals for them. I like to cook and I like my meat but all they ever give you at the food bank is pasta and more pasta! Oh, gosh. Here's my stop. Can't believe how fast the time has gone, just talking to you."

"Yes, it was nice talking to you too," I replied.

Just as Doreen was getting down the last step off the bus, I looked down at the brown paper package in my lap. "Oh, Doreen!" I called out. "Here! Take this. It's a little something I want you to have. Don't open it until you get home."

"What in the world! I couldn't!"

"Don't say anything. Just take it and enjoy!"

"Well, thank you, Ms. Patty. Have a good day!"

And do you know what? I did have a good day. After meeting Doreen, I didn't feel so sorry for myself any more. Her spirit of generosity had rubbed off on me.

Little Firecracker

by Ida May Gardiner

The little one-room school was about a mile from the house. I was given a square, pink, tin, lunch box with a peanut butter sandwich inside for later. Peanut butter sandwiches were always on the menu. I had a new jumper, new blouse, new underwear, new socks and new shoes. It felt very grown up to be heading off with the older kids and I did my best to keep up with the pace they set. They might have had to stop once, possibly twice to let me catch up. A game of pick-up softball was underway and kids joined in as they arrived on the playgrounds. Being only five, I was told I was too little to play, but I could watch.

At the ringing of the hand bell, we lined up and entered the building. I found myself next to this little blonde-haired girl at the front of the classroom. She and I were the only ones registered for Grade One that fall. When I sat at the wooden desk, my feet did not even reach the floor and I had to sit tippy-toe on my new shoes. I wondered if I would ruin them. After introductions the teacher gave us some colouring work to do while she taught the other kids. So far, I liked school. Soon the teacher asked the two of us to stand up and she would point to a word with her "pointer" stick on the black board. The first one to say the word out loud would get a point. The person who had the most points at the end would win. I was so delighted because I already knew all the important "at" words . . . mat, cat, sat, rat, fat, bat, hat. All the other children in the school room stopped their work to watch this contest. The moment the teacher announced that I had won, the other kids started booing. I sat down bewildered.

In the school yard later I found out that I was just a "dirty Indian in foster care" and needed to "learn my place". I had no idea what that meant but it sure didn't feel good. I found out that my sister, Cathy, had already had this experience and her response had been to allow these kids to say and do whatever they wanted to her without comment or complaint.

That would not be the path I would take. I was small for my age but I was also very feisty—a little firecracker on a short fuse. So when the first boy pushed me I let him have it. I didn't stop punching, kicking, and biting until they dragged me off him. I was told repeatedly by many adults that a young lady does not engaging in fist-fighting but to me the result spoke for itself. The bullies stayed away from me and there was no more booing in the classroom.

I remained an unrepentant firecracker. Somehow, through the foster care, the adoption roulette process and the 38 years of life allotted to her, my sister always managed to stay a pacifist, so in her defense, I became her firecracker too.

Mama Bee

by Kay Walker

I was born Canadian to a cowboy who married a city girl and was raised along the Bow River on a ranch in Alberta in a very good and very loving family. It was the dirty thirties when I was growing up and when I wasn't playing cowboys and Indians with my siblings I was playing in the mud. Right from the start I made pots in the mud that baked in the sun; the dirt was my clay and the sun was my kiln. Forty years later, I would have my own pottery store.

My parents were such loving parents and we lived in a small town during a time when the farm was worked by the men, but run by the women. We were cattle people. My dad had the poorest piece of the family land, but we got by. Actually I was quite spoiled—not bad spoiled, but spoiled. I was what they called a surplus child so my favorite cousin, who was the same age as me, and I got loaned out to aunts and uncles who didn't have children. We were so lucky; we were photographed by a relative who was a photographer and we got to travel, too. I was the first child in my family to go to university, so my parents were quite disappointed, when I met this railway man and one year later I was married. I left school and we moved to Saskatchewan during the Tommy Douglas dream, the dawn of Canadian health care.

The women in our small Canadian town were so giving that I had three wedding showers and got more than 24 tea cups and saucers, which was the wedding shower gift of fashion at that time. I was always more of a mug person myself being a potter and all, but my daughter still has some of those cups.

Not long after moving to the prairies my husband entered politics and I soon learned that not all families were like the beautiful one I grew up in and not all men were as good as my father. My husband was a good man, but not the father or the husband I expected. He did so much good in the community, but he ended up running with another woman. When he became an MP and it was time to move to Ottawa, I made sure he took the kids and me with him. I knew about this blond who had been after him from the start, but I wasn't going to have my kids miss out on the experience. So although things were not very happy, we all moved to Ottawa.

Shortly after he left me for her, but I had taken my kids to Expo 67 and I got to go on a parliamentary trip to Washington where I got to go into the oval office and even got to look right in the window of the space shuttle. By the end of that trip I took my wedding ring off. My husband told me not to do it then, because of appearances, but I was so sad and knew it was over long before that. The way I was raised I thought it would never come off. I had dreamed of that happy marriage and family my parents had created, but it was not to be. It was one of the hardest things I ever had to do.

Together we had two daughters and one son. Our eldest daughter was an avid skydiver with over 900 jumps, but she broke the cardinal rule and wore someone else's chute and jumped and died. It brought my husband and I closer for a little while and I am so glad that if she had to die that she died doing what she loved. She was only 23 years old. She was missed by hundreds.

Many of the skydivers even kept in touch with me. One of those skydivers helped me start my business as a potter. He knew my daughter's mother was a potter so he asked for 75 beer steins to be made because they could only serve beer on a Sunday at the drop zone if the beer was in a mug or served in a beer parlor. I was a brand new potter at the time and a girl friend of mine and I had bought a little kiln and it was in my basement. We made those mugs and everyone held a pint of beer, but they were all different shapes and sizes. That same man who asked us to make those mugs asked if we would like to go into business with him and we said "Sure, why not!" so he gave us two thousand dollars and set us up in a store at the corner of Wellington Street and Holland Avenue in Ottawa.

We called it Crossroads Canadian Fine Crafts. After two years we had paid him off and were on our own running our store. I kept the books. I didn't even really know how, but I did it. We had a wonderful experience there, met so many wonderful people. People from the embassies started buying gifts there to send as gifts internationally. I was so excited once when I learned one of my pots went to Baghdad. I didn't even know where that was then.

When my son got married I made him a 12-piece dinner set as a wedding gift. It was all I could afford then as an artist trying to make a living. He still has it and pulls it out for special occasions like Christmas dinner. I mainly made pots with embroidered silk tops and even won an award from the potter's guild for them. I got the silk from a weaver in our shop who only worked with silk. She gave me her tailings and they were always about 18 inches long. They were the perfect length for embroidery. Also at our shop all the potters would put money from their proceeds into a fund and anyone could use it to learn new things so anyone in the group could experiment. The young people were great with learning new glazes. We all benefited from that and so it was like a co-op.

We stayed open for twenty years. Now many of those young potters who started out in our shop are making a living making pottery in the region and I'm so proud of them. I still feel like they are my kids and in fact they called me Mama Bee.

The Wedding

by Michèle Gauthier

It is the Second World War. Félix has been serving overseas for the Royal Canadian Air Force in England for a few years. He left behind the love of his life, Lilianne. She is the sister of his brother Rolland's girlfriend, Simone. Rolland is also serving; he is in Scotland, a wood measurer for the Canadian Army. Félix comes from a large family of 15 kids, and he is the 13th. He revels in having a good time during his furlough; and he loves to dance. There are dances organized by the British Military with pretty young English lasses. He is very handsome, particularly in his formal uniform.

One lass has shown a steady and keen interest in Félix. He feels committed to Lilianne, although they are not engaged. There is always the sword of Damocles hanging over the military men. Will they come back after each mission, or will they perish? Is it being unfair to Lilianne to hold on to a hope that he will return to Canada, and if he returns will he be maimed for life? He is torn.

Félix consults the army chaplain for advice. What is he to do? The chaplain advises him to forget about his love back in Quebec. He is in England now and should focus on the here and now. Félix is heartbroken but the advice makes sense. He reluctantly writes to Lilianne, letting her go, wishing her all the best and starts a courtship with Tessa Guérin. She is a tall, blonde, attractive woman. She lives with her father, a dentist, and her half-sister from her mother, Nanny, who is also her step-father's dental assistant. It is a whirl-wind courtship which cumulates with a glamourous wedding ceremony just like the Hollywood movies with a guard of honour by his fellow airmen at the exit of the church along with a flyby by his fellow pilots.

There is no honeymoon; his furlough is done and he has to return to duty. Like any good French-Canadian Catholic, he followed the priest's advice. To boot, he went to the seminary, so one must follow to the letter the wishes of the Church. The priest also told him that one of the unwritten goals of having Canadian men serving abroad is for as many as possible to marry abroad, to diversify the bloodlines of the Canadian colony. He is doing his duty for his country, once by serving, twice by marrying abroad.

Félix lays awake at night on his cot; he realizes that this is a mistake, a big mistake. He is still in love with Lilianne. Tessa is not in love with him. She's in love with his uniform, with the whole glam and pomp of a military wedding, with marrying a foreigner, with the possibility of living abroad. Divorce is not an option; an annulment is practically unheard of in the Catholic church. Besides, he would be the black sheep of the family, the shame of his very religious parents, and the laughing stock of his siblings. He is trapped.

War Stories

The Whim

by Ted MacTaggart

As we age and look back on life, we tend to attribute our good life to the wise decisions we made after thinking things through and coming to a reasonable conclusion about the paths we should take. I'm sure that most folks would agree that we must think wisely and clearly about any action that will affect our future well being.

Well folks, I must plead guilty to not following those common sense opinions. Rather, I shaped my future by acting on a whim.

When I was a young man of 16 years of age I joined the reserve army and served in an anti-aircraft artillery unit. When I was 18, a couple of my pals convinced me that I should join The Regimental Band so we could have a few beers at the end of the evening, after completing some basic training.

At that stage of my life it was very attractive to be able to play (not all that well) a little military music and then socialize with my pals, who also enjoyed some beer.

For two weeks in the summer the regiment was deployed to a firing range just outside of Victoria, B.C. We all took the train from Winnipeg to Victoria and trained on the guns that were designed to shoot enemy aircraft down. The results of course depended on our ability to follow the drills properly. The Air Force towed targets behind their aircraft and when we weren't doing too well at bringing them down, they would remind us that they were towing them not pushing them.

It was at that training area that I went along with about six other guys on a whim.

We had finished the training for the day. The next day was Sunday so no live firing would take place. We had decided that this would be a good night to enjoy some beer. While we were enjoying ourselves, one of the guys spoke up saying, "Hey guys, this is great. Let's join the regular army." There were cheers and shouts of, "Yah, let's!" and two went along with the whim. I had put zero thought into what the consequences would be for myself. There is a big difference between spending one evening a week in the army and spending seven days a week for fifty-two weeks of the year.

The commanding officer was informed the next day that members of his reserve were planning on going regular. He did his very best to speed up the steps to get us into the regular force.

In the regular force we were put through basic training, sent to units and quickly learned what it was all about.

I consider myself very lucky to have answered the whim. spent 35 years in the military and I enjoyed all of it. I have, however, always tried to remember that I wouldn't always get the right "whim"; so I try now to always think things through.

It Has Been a Great Life

by George Squance

There was a requirement for engineering types in the RCN, and after some consideration, I decided to sign on for a five-year hitch. I went to Ennis More Gardens in London, England for an interview with a liaison staff member who was a senior engineering officer. Twelve years' experience in marine engineering was just what was required. It took three months to sell my house in Davenport, so I was hired on as a fitter in the dockyard with a gang of former naval mechanics.

As soon as my house sold, I sailed for St John New Brunswick with my wife and infant son in tow, and a guaranteed job. We were on Empress of France from Liverpool U.K. to St. John. From there, we crossed by ferry to Digby and on to Halifax, by train, where we stayed at the Carleton Hotel (it was purchased many years later by Atlantic Chiefs and Petty Officers Association). We obtained an apartment to rent at Lakefront (Maynard's Lake, Dartmouth, Nova Scotia) and I was duly posted to a leadership course at Cornwallis base to become "Canadianised".

Then came my draft to HMCS Algonquin. That was a fairly pleasant experience although it was away from home and family. Following refit, it seemed as though we were never in home port. It came as a relief to be posted to HMCS Cape Breton which was then permanently alongside as a training facility for artificer apprentices. We decided to deploy from Cape Breton to the west coast. I became a member of the steaming party involved in scrambling to get everything operational, which was duly accomplished.

I have inadvertently omitted a period here in the early 1960s when both the HMCS Lanark and the HMCS Cayuga spent separate summers on the Great Lakes—up the seaway all the way to Thunder Bay, "head-of-the-lakes"(formerly the two cities of Fort William and Port Arthur)—almost two-thousand miles inland from Halifax and families. The purpose was the training of Naval Reservists from the various "Divisions". It meant to be away from home port from May to September, back in time to go on N.A.T.O exercises in European waters until late December. The journey traversing the various locks of the St. Lawrence Seaway was interesting, although quite boring at times.

During summer inland, Canada became quite warm, frequently in the 30s Celsius. We were given the opportunity to go on a brewery tour; the first one filled quickly and by the time we returned the tour was over. There was still time to join in on the hospitality though. Everywhere we went the natives were very friendly and hospitable.

Many operations were known as chequers. We would be at sea for monthly periods, looking for Russian submarines, and coming into harbour to avoid paying crews extra. A weekend in harbour was taken up with making good any defects, so outings with the kids and wife were rare. This is life in the real navy!

Later I was posted to HMCS Cayuga, a tribal class destroyer, undergoing refit at Halifax shipyards. Next I became an instructor at Stadacoma barracks engineering school. As a result I became a part of our submarine service, back in 1965. Shortly after, I was posted back to Halifax to join our Canadian sub, Ojibwa. Ojibwa had recently crossed the Atlantic Ocean submerged in snort mod and was a bit of a show piece around the east coast. We did a lot of sea time on her.

During the 1970s, I was visiting Ontario as frequently as possible to see my son in the Mounties (RCMP). My daughter had also moved to Ontario working as a laboratory technician. Both my children had been educated for several years in England where their mother had been resident. I decided to leave Nova Scotia and move to Ontario in 1978.

I soon obtained employment at York University, Toronto, as a millwright. Work there was a piece of cake. The next six years were permeated with excellent camaraderie. It was my first exposure to unionized work environments. My workmates got together to hold a wonderful party in honour of my retirement. I retired from there at the early age of 64.

Money I derived was used to finance my trip around the world where I visited many places that I never managed to see while in Naval service. That included Tahj Mahal in India, Thailand temples, a bit of China, Hong Kong, Japan, and Pearl Harbour in Hawaii. Since then I have visited Egypt's pyramids and tombs, the former Yugoslavia, and travelled around Russia. Back home again in North America, to cap it all off, I rode my touring motorcycle across Canada and USA from coast to coast at age 75. Australia and South Africa were revisited in 1997.

It has been a great life. My greatest hope now is to be around a little while longer and to be forever grateful for each dawn of another day.

My Father, My Hero

by Michèle Gauthier

I remember Félix Gauthier, my father, my hero

He was born 20 days after the declaration of the First World War in a small Charlevoix country village of St. Irenée. He was the thirteenth child of Sir Irène Gauthier and Lady Herméline Girard, proprietors of a large land in the St. Pierre concession road with a bird's eye view of the St. Lawrence River. Godchild of his eldest sister, Marie, he grew up with her and her family, down the road, with his parents in Shelter Bay and he did his classical studies at the Bathurst Seminary in New Brunswick.

An avid hockey player, he impressed all by his speed and his prowess which foiled his competitors, even those who had a stronger build and were slower.

As a young 25-year-old bachelor, he enrolled voluntarily in the military service, when the Second World War was declared, with one of his older brothers, Rolland. If one enrolled voluntarily, one could choose which part of the military to belong to and which training to receive; if conscripted, there was no choice. They did their training in Borden, Manitoba, and in Trenton, Ontario before being deployed overseas.

Rolland was in the army; he was a forester and would be measuring wood in Scotland for building warships. Félix was in the Royal Canadian Air Force. He was a pilot, a navigator and an aeronautical mechanic. The airforce's motto is *Per Ardua, ad Astra—In adversity, reach for the stars.* He would carry this motto throughout his life.

He was in exile from his country for six years, when he was deployed to England, India and Burma. For his military service, he received four medals: the Canadian Medal for voluntary service, the Defense Medal, the 1939-1945 War Medal and the Cross of Burma.

Two French-Canadian brothers went to war to defend the freedom of others and preserve it for their peers. Under a shining star, when a multitude of their fellows died under arms, they both returned to their native country. We are honoured that Dad is still with us at the venerable age of 98. He is of the generation of heros who rarely talk of their military prowess, too much pain for their fallen colleagues, too much horror seen, but he remembers.

It would take two generations before another family member of the Gauthier family wore the colours of our country in active military service to protect their loved ones and all others in war time, military conflict and peace.

Sometime after the war, Félix returned to Canada and worked for Canadair in the construction of airplanes. The call to duty returned seven years later.

In 1949 and 1953 respectively, the Soviet Union detonated its first hydrogen and plutonium bombs. The Soviet bombers could now launch nuclear bombs and reach the industrial centers and population clusters of North America.

In 1952, Canada was threatened by Soviet invasion by land, sea or bomb. We participated in the creation of the DEW Line (Distant Early Warning) to protect Canada and the United States against Soviet invasion. It was the most ambitious project undertaken in the Canadian Arctic. Its creation would also mark the turning point for the maintenance of Canadian sovereignty in the Arctic. The DEW line is a network of 63 radar stations along the 69th parallel, approximately 250 kilometers from the Arctic Circle, which spreads from Alaska to Baffin Island and covers more than 10,000 kilometers. Like a pearl necklace, these isolated stations comprised a radar system in the Arctic tundra where brave men do surveillance against possible attacks by Soviet bombers and to give a warning in case of land or sea invasion. It is the biggest technological project in the Canadian Arctic which employed nearly 25,000 people.

In December 1954, Félix was among a select group of brave men who left for the polar circle to live and work in primitive conditions to ensure the construction and the maintenance of these radar stations. There were no roads; the men were dropped off by military planes in the arid tundra, in the eternal winter darkness with a few dogs, tents, skidoos, fuel and food supply. They had to work in temperatures so cold that they had never been registered before and for which no ordinary thermometers could record. The majority of the work was done during the long winters, in frigid temperatures, on a soil covered by permafrost and ice and in total darkness, thus in the most hostile and isolated part of North America.

During the short summers of 1955, 1956 and 1957, when the ice did not cover the Arctic Ocean and when a passage was open, military ships brought food supplies and building materials necessary for the construction of the stations. In 1958, the DEW line became the cornerstone of the North American Aerospace Defense Command (NORAD).

Félix worked on the DEW Line for many years, without saying a word to anyone about this work that was confidential. No one will find any reference of this in his curriculum vitae, just the time frame with the reference "odd jobs in the North". The gap of those years exiled from his native Charlevoix and his family to continue to protect his country and his fellow Canadians against the Cold War menace between the United States and the USSR, the nuclear attacks and the protection of Canadian sovereignty in the Arctic remains unexplained.

A memorandum found in his personal papers in 2012 shows that he had a secret security clearance from the Canadian Department of National Defence and that he received isolation pay which confirms his service for this perilous work. Again, he has never mentioned the enormous responsibility he assumed, preferring to tell effervescent anecdotes of his mush dog team, the unforgettable nights of aurora borealis shows, of the stark beauty of the Arctic nature and of the tranquility of this barren land. But he remembers.

I remember and thank my father, Félix Gauthier, my uncle Rolland Gauthier, my cousin Rollande Gauthier as well as my friends Bernard Lecours and Marilyn Greene who served our country and have given so much in the name of peace and freedom. We remember and we love you.

Depression Era

A Dangerous Practice

by Ruth Knapp

In the early 1930s, before Newfoundland became a part of Canada, there was a young man named Noel Stuart Knapp, who, upon graduating as a doctor from Queen's University in Kingston, Ontario, found himself recently married, penniless and without a job. Therefore, when a remote community on the Southeast coast of Newfoundland offered him not only a job but also a house and $2000 dollars in his pocket as soon as he and his new wife stepped off the boat at Harbour Briton, Noel accepted with gratitude. Consequently, Dr. Knapp became the first doctor to practice in that isolated area.

Life in Newfoundland in those days was both primitive and harsh; no roads came in or went out of Harbour Briton. The only access was by boat or bi-weekly steamer.

Noel and Leah's house, like all the others in the village, had no electricity, received water from a deep well, and coal oil lamps provided necessary light in the evenings. In fact, during Dr. Knapp's year of practice, he often had to carry out procedures including operations by flashlight, assisted by his young son or his wife.

One day, shortly after Dr.Knapp had arrived, a fisherman knocked on his door. He had come by boat from a few miles away to inform the doctor that his wife was about to give birth. And so, black bag in hand, Dr. Knapp left on his first medical adventure.

Although a severe storm was brewing, the doctor knew he had to answer this call immediately. He and the distressed father-to-be,

Mr. Ezra Stone, climbed aboard a small boat and headed to an island called, Sagona, a few miles out to sea. In spite of gale-force winds and high waves slashing the sides of the boat, the courageous pair made it safely to the island. Despite the primitive conditions, no running water and no electricity, by boiling water on top of a wood stove, this young doctor was able to bring a bouncing baby boy safely into the world just before the vicious storm broke. Due to the intensity of this storm, Dr. Knapp was stranded in that home for four days before the young father was able to return the good doctor to his home. He left his poor wife, Leah at home holding her breath wondering whether he was alive or dead.

Before leaving, the baby's dad asked Dr. Knapp what he owed him for delivering the bundle of joy. As Dr. Knapp looked around the one room shack, he felt sorry for these poor people who seemed to be eking out a meager living. The doctor's usual fee was $25 in spite of the dangers and hardship he encountered along the way. In this case Dr. Knapp thought, maybe he shouldn't charge so much. So finally he said, "Could you spare $5?" To which the dad answered "Sure, Doc". With that, Mr. Stone reached under the bed and pulled out a huge bag filled with solid gold coins. After spreading them out on the cold floor, he rooted through them until he found a small $5 gold coin which he proudly gave to the doctor. Upon reflection, Dr. Knapp realized that there was probably $10,000.00 worth of gold pieces in that bag.

However, the good doctor's efforts were to be rewarded soon in a very unique way as the baby boy he had brought into the world was named "Noel Stuart Knapp Stone", in Dr. Knapps honour.

In our own family, this special "trail blazer" was known, fondly as "Papa". Our family is very proud of his many accomplishments in the forefront of the practice of medicine in Newfoundland as he served for over 25 years, in Harbor Briton, Gander Airport and Lewisport, healing the sick, bringing many new lives into this world as well as saving others, while often risking his own. It was a vital, but dangerous practice. Thank you, Papa.

A 1931 Romance

by Margaret Amyotte

Sitting in his arm chair, Jeremy gently put his newspaper and glasses down, and stared at his bride of fifty years, saying. "You are more beautiful now than the first time we met."

Stunned, Lita blushed, and with a cunning smile answered, "Thank you, Dear. Keep your glasses off. You too, Dear, are more handsome," as she stared at him, with her glasses down the bridge of her nose. They both started laughing as they reminisced.

It was 1930, the year of the Great Depression. Considering the state of the economy, agriculture seemed to be the government's primary source of revenue. Therefore, the government granted parcels of land in Northern Quebec to families without work. Joe Boland had just moved his family from Massachusetts, where he owned a mill, to Montreal. Unable to provide for his family, he applied for such a grant. Also from Montreal, Alex Tallen, who was in the same predicament, had applied for the same grant, which included some money, necessary tools, and means to get to the destination. Their destination was in a rural place, in the Temiskamingue district, which was called Remigny. Those courageous men arrived first to clear the land and build log cabins, before sending for their wives and families. From morn, till night, they toiled and cultivated the land to sustain their families. From the oldest to the youngest, they all shared the work. After a week of hard work, each family took turns having a house party. Most of them were very musical, and entertained themselves with storytelling, dancing, singing, eating, and being merry.

My mother and father were strong, secure parents of four children, two girls and two boys, all born within six years. They had a set division of duties. Mother ran a spotless house with daily domestic help and generally set the rules of discipline for us. She was a caring mother but demanding and expected us to respect her wishes. She worried constantly about what the neighbors thought and instilled that idea in our heads. It helped create guilt. I really thought the neighbors were going about their own destructive mayhem and didn't give a damn about us but still I complied.

Mother always welcomed our friends and an extra plate at the dinner table or a sleepover were common events. She was also always pleased if I were going out. I was nearly 17 by then and in university so there were many tea dances and formals to which I was invited. As a matter of fact, at that moment, dates and dances were far more important to me than academics. Mother never set a curfew which delighted and puzzled me. I was the envy of my friends. I thought that she trusted me but I knew that if I broke that trust she would be very disappointed, so I was very careful not to act out.

Dad, a most caring and quiet man, ran his mill business from early in the morning until supper-time six days a week, rang the church bell every Sunday for our weekly service at the Universalist Church and tended his large vegetable garden nightly. We had a prodigious number of fresh vegetables during the summer, plus potatoes and all root vegetables stored in the root cellar for the winter.

The depression was still hanging over all, but we ate well and I was proud of my dad, who rather than cut back on workers in the mill, cut our level of family income to theirs to keep everybody working. One day, as Mother was sweeping the front steps leading down to the road, the wife of Dad's teamster walked by and stuck her foot up to show a hole in the bottom of the shoe. "See what your husband makes me wear!" she said. My mother stuck her own shoe up to show similar wear. "We're all in the same boat, Marion," she said. And so we were.

Tramps came to the door quite frequently. Dad said we must have been marked as a good place to stop. They came at noon hour, which was our big meal, and Mother or Dad would always invite them in to eat with us. I was a little nervous and I noticed Yvonne, our hired girl, sitting on the edge of her chair which made me feel safer. She was a big, hefty girl who once, when Karl stepped on her newly polished floor, picked up all 6 ft. of him off the ground and heaved him over the veranda rail. I felt she could handle the tramps if the need arose. Sometimes my mother packed lunches for a hungry tramp. Once we watched a man check his lunch and then throw it in the river. I guess he didn't like sardine sandwiches.

Karl was a tease! He played jokes on Mother, Dad, my sister Jean, brother Ross and me. He called Mother, whose name was Alice, Alice MacKenzie, a suspected victim of Jack the Ripper. It always seemed to please her. If my Dad was on the phone with a business client, Karl would pile hats on his head and coats on his back. Dad never let on but finished his business and then shrugged off the coats and hats—but he always had a smile on his face. At the dining table Karl teased me constantly by referring to boys that I knew. He could always make me blush. One time I threw a boiled potato at him. It missed him and hit the wall behind him. My mother reprimanded me for making a mess. Practical jokes can be fun but also a pain at times, I thought to myself. That day I excused myself from the table and went to my room—but I was smiling.

I was in university and Karl was in his last year of high school. I had established my sibling priority temporarily. I opened my diary and recorded this small triumph. All was well in our world as I wrote in my diary on Sept. 15, 1935.

World War II began in 1939. Karl, who had never liked school, enlisted in 1940. As he said, "If I don't go now, how will I ever see the world?" He was in a bomber as a wireless air gunner when he was shot down over Sicily in 1941. He was reported missing and my parents went through a whole year of hoping that he was still alive before the whole crew was declared dead. Years later, I remember my mother, who was in the last days of her life, telling me that when Karl was declared missing she caught a case of the wrinkles and never recovered. I have missed his teasing, and will for the rest of my life.

A Tin House in a Small Town

by Gail Casselman

In 1938, I was born in a tin house with a tin roof in a very small Ontario town. I was the second youngest of six children; five girls and one boy. I was brought into this world in this house by our town doctor who attended the birth of all the children within a forty-mile radius. The house had four small bedrooms upstairs, several rooms downstairs and a cellar with a cistern and an earthen floor. Oh how I hated it when my mother sent me to get vegetables or preserves from the cellar. It was cold and damp, and I was sure something terrible lurked in the dark corners.

We had no running water and no central heating but we did have electricity and a crank up telephone on the wall. No one had a private telephone line. Six or seven people shared that line so you had to be careful what you said as anyone on the shared line could listen to your conversation. As there was no water in the house, we had to use the outdoor toilets in the summer and something like a portable toilet in the winter. Once a week the portable toilet was put outside by the road and the "honey wagon" came around to empty it. I never knew or asked where the contents of this "honey wagon" ended up.

I loved laying on my bed and listening to the rain on the tin roof and playing cut-out dolls with my sister. Our cut-out dolls and everything else came from the Eaton catalogue. We had lots of fun, using our imagination to give our cut-out dolls a very nice life. From the upstairs, there was a very wide open staircase going to the main floor. I would stand at the top and think I could fly down. I fell many times but was really heartbroken when I fell and broke the only real doll I ever had.

As with most houses in this time, we had a summer kitchen. Every spring we scrubbed and cleaned it, and then moved the living essentials into the summer kitchen as it was basically where we lived for the summer. Between the summer kitchen and the winter dinner area of the main house was a large cabinet where all the dishes and pots and pans were kept. It had doors opening into the summer kitchen and on the other side, a door opening into the winter eating area. Twice a year everything in this cupboard had to be rearranged to put the most used equipment closest to either the winter dining area or the summer kitchen.

I loved that summer kitchen. It had an old couch with many cushions and I spent hours and hours reading comic books there. Also, this was where the ritual of the weekly bath was held. A large old tin tub was brought into the kitchen. The water was heated on the wood stove and we took turns getting into the tub. As I was the youngest, I was the last in the tub and by then the water was not warm or very fresh.

There was a wood stove, an ice box, a sink and a hand pump in the inside kitchen and a sink and pump in the summer kitchen. I still remember going to the outside pump to get water. Although I was too young to remember this, one of my older sisters recently told me this story. One night my mother saw a man getting water from the outside pump. She brought the man in the house, fed him and let him sleep on our downstairs couch for the night. She warned the kids not to come downstairs in the morning until she called them. Early in the morning she gave the man a coat and something to eat and sent him on his way. It turned out that as she suspected, he was an escaped German prisoner of war and was trying to get across the St. Lawrence River to the U.S.A. When asked later why she did that, she said that he was just a boy, very cold and hungry. It seems to me that she could have got in a lot of trouble for helping an escaped POW!

Behind the summer kitchen was a wood shed which had a long straight ladder, attached to the wall, going up to a sort of attic. This was another place where I spent a lot of time in the summer. There were things like furniture and boxes that needed to be explored but the best part was the thrill of climbing up and down that scary ladder.

My mother was a very strong willed person and during the time my father was away at war, she worked long hours to provide for her family. She worked for a short while at a restaurant in town and then ran a hair salon out of our house. She had to pump and heat the water to wash hair. There was one of those hair dryers that had a top that looked like an upside down bowl in the room where she did hair. Long wires hung down from this bowl and at the end of the wires there were metal clamps used to curl hair. This apparatus looked to me like something from a torture chamber.

This little tin house in this little town was surrounded by farmland, fields and, what seemed to me to be a large forest. I was free to spend a good amount of time wandering around the fields and bush with our dog, Rex. I am sure it is this small town background and the freedom to explore that instilled the love that I have for all our great Canadian outdoors.

The Flu

by Caroline O'Leary-Hartwick

Grandmother, who was a ninth-generation descendant of Acadian heritage, was interested in doing things well. Gert, for that was her nickname from Gertrude, would not put up with sloppy work and she was known far and wide for her skill. She was also very frugal and knew how to make a little go a long way with style. She loved her farm animals as they were in a lot of ways her pets. Her sheep had the best coats, which were spun into the most superior wool that was sought by many. Her chickens were well cared for and produced delicious eggs that amazed many with their bright colour and scrumptious flavour. Many sought her out to buy her wares as they knew they were getting quality, as well as a bright smile and a cup of tea with mouth-watering homemade bread and butter.

One of Gert's favorite pastimes was to go picking berries with a friend or two. She would set in the middle of a blueberry patch with her wide apron on her lap and contently pick blueberries, as the saying goes, till the cows came home. At the end of a productive day she would come home with buckets of freshly picked, wild, Nova Scotia blueberries. She sold her stash to the blueberry man, as we all knew him, Mr. George. All us children thought he was a clown with his wide blue mouth, big red cheeks, his hat though red was smeared in blue, and his hand appeared to have very skin-like blue gloves. He loved getting Gert's blueberries as they were the cleanest he had ever purchased and always gave Gert extra for it. No one knew what she did with the money!

Now, our house in rural Nova Scotia was sturdily made but not well insulated from the fierce winters blowing off the Chedabucto Bay, so preparation had to be made to insure for some type of comfort. Having done almost all his preparation, Gert's husband, Fon, busily set about finishing his tasks. This meant setting up the extra stove in the hallway and beginning the fires to eliminate the late fall evening chills. He busily set about installing the pipe and preparing and cleaning the dampers, filling the wood box and other such tasks the job required.

Meanwhile, Gert was down at her lowly chicken coop ensuring her treasured chickens were protected during the coming winter and continued to produce the valued eggs. She was busy going about her chores, when she smelled smoke; perplexed she came out of the coop, looked up and saw smoke coming out of the flu. "NO!" she screeched.

Flying out of the chicken pen, holding onto the ends of her apron, she galloped up to the house. Still holding onto her apron, she stumbled, panting and puffing into the kitchen, bellowing; "NO, Fon, NO, for God's sake, me monies in the flu!" He looked at her all red faced huffing and puffing and burst out laughing. Gert was not impressed as she rushed to put out the fire before any damage was done. Fon put on a pair of her hand knitted mitts and dismantled the now hot pipes and put his hand into the flu, and low and behold, there was her stash of money that she had collected over the spring and summer from all her frugal endeavors.

The Value of Community

The Village on the Hill

by Carol Mathieu

Years ago, when I was young, there were houses up the road from my parent's farm and we called it the Village on the Hill.

In the winter months, my father would hitch the team of horses onto his homemade snow plough. The plough was made of wood and was V-shaped. I can remember it had three pieces of wood in the middle of the plough. I suppose it was to hold the outside wood in place.

My dad would plough from the main road up to the houses on the hill. If he didn't plough, it might be days before we got out. I always tried to go with him. If I went, I had to sit in the middle seat and hold on tight to the wood. My feet had to be up on the wood board.

My mother was scared that I would fall. I can remember my father letting me hold the reins and I thought it was the greatest thing, and when we finished ploughing, I would run into the house and tell my sister that I drove the horses.

My mother would always get upset with my father saying, "Mike, she can get hurt." But I can remember my father and his big smile and putting his finger to his mouth and looking at me with a grin.

Some of the people on the hill had to work and the only means of transportation at that time for them was a bicycle or walking; there were a few who might have had old cars Some of the younger ones hitched a ride on my father's snow plough, to get to a bus which was quite a distance from all the houses, and, of course, we had to attend school.

We were fortunate as we had root cellars; my father would dig a big hole in the ground and fix steps into it which he covered with mud, boards, straw or hay. We had large gardens and my father sold some of the crop to the grocery store on Bank St. We always had enough for the winter months with our crop of vegetables and our apple trees. I hated the parsnips. We also had our own meat and every Sunday we would have a roast of pork.

My mother would make cheese and we drank the fresh milk right from the cow and never got sick. My mother would put cream into a large glass jar and make me shake the jar or roll it back and forth, and I would make butter that was so sweet. Now I think she did this to keep me out of trouble.

My mother must have been one of the pioneers for women who started working outside the home. She also helped with the farm work. It must have been a hard time for them as she kept two jobs while my father worked for the city.

On our many trips up the hill, my mother, who was a great baker, delivered many loaves of bread to some of her friends. Some families had ten to fourteen in the family.

A lot of the families tried to make a living but with that many people to feed it was hard to keep up. In the winter months, my dad delivered the bread or buns my mother baked.

When he took the bread into the house, I was allowed to hold the reins on the horses even though I'm sure the horses would never have moved unless my father was there.

Some of the houses on the hill had tar paper covering the boards to keep the snow, cold and wind out. When I would ask my father why they covered their houses with paper, he would always say that these were good people who didn't have much and they had to keep warm.

One of the houses on the hill always fascinated me as it was the best up on the hill. This house was a big house covered in white board with a big veranda. What I liked most about this house was the big swing in the yard. The man who owned the house was always away. My father said the owner worked for the railway. Dad always waved to say hello when we went by this house. The older children from this house lived and worked in the city for the government and the railway. They were better off than most up on the hill.

When it was warm weather my mother would take me with her when she went up the hill. We would walk and, at nearly every house, we stopped and she talked to the people.

Most of the houses had gardens to keep them alive and eating in the winter months. Some of the homes were lucky if they had coal furnaces but a lot of the houses were heated with wood.

I went to school with some of these kids. Some were so poor that in the winter they wore running shoes or rubber boots in the snow. Being a child I never thought any different about this.

We were not rich but my mother was good at making clothes. She would alter some of the hand-me-downs from my sister's clothes. She would make dresses if she had the material and also suits for my father. From the flour bags she made all her dish towels and aprons.

Most of the people on the hill worked but a lot were let go from their jobs once winter came. Some of the men worked for a company who had green houses and large gardens that grew vegetables for the big grocery stores.

Most of the people up on that hill went to church on Sunday when they could get out.

My father taught us all how to work the gardens, how to weed by hand and how to milk a cow.

I remember when I went with my mother for our walk up the hill about one particular family. This family lived in a little tar-paper house, with a dirt floor. These people looked old to me but when I asked someone later on in life, they said that this couple were in their forties. What I remember most were the chickens running around the house, and how this lady was always wearing a long dress with an apron, and when the man rode his bicycle, he sat up as straight as a board. They had no electricity and a wood stove sat in the middle of the floor.

This couple were, I believe, Ukrainian because my parents are Ukrainian and my mother could speak Russian, Polish and, of course, Ukrainian. The man from this house wanted my mother to buy him a radio so he gave her the money and she bought the radio. When we went on our walk the next week, she brought him his radio and she showed him how to turn it off and on. That night the man came to our house and told my father that my mother got him a radio that does not speak English. Apparently, the radio was tuned to a French station and he didn't know enough to turn the channel. So my father told him the radio was alright but he had to turn the dial.

My mother and father were very kind, generous people. I can remember one Christmas when I was given a doll. She was so big with golden ringlets but there was only one shoe on the doll. I can remember crying and crying. I didn't want her because Santa forgot to give her two shoes. My father took me outside and said to look up—see in the sky, there goes Santa Claus. He forgot the shoe but will bring it back next year.

Santa was too far away to bring the shoe back. Well, to this day at Christmas I still look up and remember what my father said and actually I think I see the sleigh and Santa.

With all the houses up on the hill, we had the United Nations of languages living there. People were of English, French, Italian, Polish, Russian and Ukrainian descent. My mother was very gifted as she could speak Ukrainian, her mother tongue, Russian, Polish a little French and Italian—all this with no formal education.

The people on that hill were hard working people

Our farm property went from our home to the top of the hill. At the back end of our property my father pastured the animals. The property had a creek that ran through it. The property was kind of hilly. Some of the younger boys who lived on the hill would dam the creek and I'm sure my brother was involved in that because he went to school with the boys on the hill and they were all friends.

I think this is where they learned to swim. I don't remember much of this as I was much younger than my brother. I did ask someone how deep it was and they said at some places it was at least ten feet deep. I do remember my mother telling my sister and me not to go there alone. She told me that one time I fell in the creek and nearly drowned and the dog we had pulled me out of the creek.

I can remember years later when I was a little older, my father sitting on a bench outside our house. There were two men from up on the hill; one was an Italian man who spoke very little English and the other gentleman was Russian and my father who was Ukrainian. They were all talking to each other and none of them really understood English that well. My father would say something and the Italian man would say "Sure, sure, Mike that right." I know they understood what each one was saying because they had that kind of communication between friends.

I still speak to one of the ladies who lived in the big home on the hill. Her sister is ninety-eight years old and she is in her late eighties and both have better memories than mine.

Years later, all that property was expropriated to make room for a highway and park.

There is much more to this story but this is what my mind will let me remember at this time.

Harvest Bee Memories

by Sylvia Findlay

When I was a prairie kid, threshing time, the culmination of summer's arduous labor and constant concern, was an exciting event. Neighbors and family pooled their energy, workforce and resources to insure all were able to bring in the harvest before winter set in. The threshing machine belonged to family and neighbors; the tractor was owned by Dad and his brother Mike, and everyone donated four-hoofed horsepower and hay racks to transfer the sheaves to the threshing machine.

The women, chattering and gossiping, helped each other with food preparation. Apple, lemon and raisin pies were baked, chickens and pork roasted, vegetables scraped and mounds of homemade bread cooled on the oilcloth-covered tables. The annual event took on a party atmosphere. One family trying to do all on their own would have felt defeated but the group felt exhilarated. We children were pumped! There was excitement in the air. It was great fun getting underfoot, watching our mothers prepare to take the lunch or supper out to the field.

Dozens of sandwiches were slapped together for the ravenous laborers. Massive amounts of tea brewed; a cider made from cordial syrup and fresh, spine-tingling, cold well-water was stirred together and poured into quart sealers. The horse hitched to the buggy; food, plates and cutlery loaded, Mother flicked the reins and at a slow amble drove the feast across the golden stubble to the threshing machine site. We children scampered excitedly alongside in an attempt to be there first.

What a picnic we enjoyed! Friendship flowed; little kids, including me, basked in the attention and gratitude expressed by the famished men and boys, as we passed the sandwiches around and ran to get more cider. Mother and the Aunts were wonderful cooks. Roast chicken has never again been as delicious as in my childhood, shared with a group of grimy, hungry men.

Our crop harvested; the entire gang moved on to the next fully ripened field on the adjoining farm where the routine began all over again. The excitement was exhilarating but short lived. Some of the grain was delivered to the local elevator in Vista, to be shipped to Eastern Canada for export; the remainder was kept stored in granaries until market dictated, nailed shut from mice and skunks. Then it was time for each individual household to buckle down to prepare their home and outbuildings for the long lonely arduous winter.

I really loved harvest time; it just went by much too quickly.

Serious Business

by Caroline O'Leary-Hartwick

"Take that you old coot!" he roared and threw a card down on the table with such force the whole table shook. With a cigarette dangling from his lip and smoke trailing up into his eyes, he simply smiled with a twinkle in his eye and threw down another card, everyone around the table giggled. To my left a flash caught my eye as a hand came down hard on another table nearby, "Beat that you old fart!" was spewed out . Everyone sitting down at the table looked very intent. I slid past the hot stove, upon which the kettle was merrily bubbling, and crept up to the back of a chair at the table, "Mommy, can I watch?" I stammered. "Go! Scoot! Go help Ruby in the pantry!" With my head down, eyeing the kids sitting in the corner, on the floor playing a string game and hearing the hooting coming from the room beyond them, I edged myself around the room to the pantry. My aunt and several other women were bustling around putting food on plates, "Can I have a cookie?" I squeaked. "Things aren't ready yet. Here, put these neatly on this plate, and don't eat any!" came the barked reply.

There wasn't any television back then and this was the highlight of the adult entertainment—The Saturday night 45's card play! Anyone that enjoyed playing cards looked forward to these evenings in the country. A collection of prizes were accepted from card players and non-card-players alike, to support the event. The card plays were held at a different house every other Saturday night; this was done to support the local Catholic Church. However, as I remember, that was where the religion began and ended. There were people that came for the socializing, some came to drink and have fun and play a game of cards and then there were the diehard card players. My grandmother was one of those and this was serious business. She wasn't happy sitting at a table where folks were laughing and having fun. You had to pay attention to what you were doing. She was there to win!

Often times they would play long into the night and in some cases the next morning. The diehard players would play for anything, it really didn't matter, and it was the winning that was the prize. They were interesting times those Saturday nights, watching the adults become very different people than the ones you saw during an ordinary day.

Gertrude loved playing cards; she seldom missed a card play. Even if she was very ill, just mention playing a game of cards and she was right there just drooling to begin. There was always a twinkle in her eye at the prospect of playing cards, but once she picked up the cards the joking was over and it was down to the business of winning.

Card playing was serious business then and still is with some people. They wouldn't miss a game.

Pregnant and Mired in Mud

by Ruth Knapp

Beautiful, mild spring weather always makes children restless, chatty and more rambunctious. At the time the adult world experiences a certain inner anxious feeling often called "Spring Fever". This year was no exception. The spring thaw had come early and quickly. Being a teacher meant that days were fun but tiring.

In the spring of '59, I was also pregnant which added to my anxious and tired state; to make things even more hectic, we had just moved into our new dream home at the end of February. We were thrilled with the house, but I was experiencing a lot of Morning Sickness which lasted all day; may I assure you the new smells in the house did not help my digestion. Needless to say, my world was a little frenetic.

On this particular day in early March, I was in a terrible hurry when I left school at four o'clock, because I had to head right down town to the National System of Baking to pick up my husband's favorite pie and my favorite cookies. We were having company over for dinner and we could get these articles nowhere else but this fabulous bakery on Bank Street in downtown Ottawa.

As I had ordered these baked goods a couple of days previously, the young girl had no trouble finding them in the back room. One of the symbols of the National System of Baking that set them apart was the use of the pure white square light cardboard boxes in which they parceled almost every item of baking they sold. This made the baking easy to be stacked and recognized; a good advertisement for their store.

As I said earlier, Bob and I had just moved into our precious new home in a brand new suburb called, BelAir Heights. In February, when we moved into this new subdivision, the streets were not paved but they were hardened mud. They had not yet been scraped, rolled or filled with crushed stone, so they were little better than muddy lanes. However, once the spring thaw had come, in March, they became literally quagmires. In fact, those of us who had moved in earlier were barely able to get our furniture moved in before the roads literally became impassable.

Consequently, we were forced to park our cars about a block and a half away, outside the actual subdivision, and walk in. We were forced to wear rubber boots at all times and to leave our muddy boots in our automobiles each day. Fortunately, we were all young and venturesome. However, being pregnant and nauseated most of the time made my emotions close to the surface. I was not pleased to have to be plodding through this mud, daily, to get to my new home.

On this particular afternoon, I got out of the car, wearing my favorite, beautiful, light brown coat with the gorgeous fox fur collar, only to have to turn around and put on my horrible muddy boots and, of course, pick up the precious baking. Then began my difficult trek through the mire. As I trudged my way along the first block, holding my baking up in front of my chest, I realized that the mud around me was becoming deeper and harder to plow through with every step. As I would put one foot down, it would sink almost up to the top of the boot! I seemed to be literally in quicksand! I just knew that I was going to die right there on my own street. The quicksand was going to swallow me up. Due to holding my baking, which suddenly did not seem so delectable, I could not use my hands to pick up my boots; I was literally stuck in the mud. I figured I was going to sink and never be found. It was not long before sheer panic set in.

Just as I was about to give up on life and sit down and let the quicksand swallow all of us—myself and my unborn child and the baking—I looked up in desperation and saw a lady standing in her picture window. As she waved at me, she gave me some hope. At least somebody would know what happened to me and the exact position of where I had drowned in this muddy abyss. And so, I took heart and literally maneuvered each boot and somehow I managed to get past that corner which was the worst and thus I eventually reached the safety of our home. Needless to say, I phoned our friends and cancelled the dinner party. We could not expect our friends to trudge through that quagmire.

The next day I heard that friends of ours who lived on the next street had come into the subdivision a short while after my little adventure, carrying their little two-year-old on his dad's shoulders. All three of them fell headlong into the muddy mess. They had to throw out all of their clothing and I guess they, too, found it quite frightening.

As a result of our pioneering, our city, Ottawa, passed a by-law forbidding builders to move people into their homes until the roads have been filled with crushed stone or finished so that no one has to live through the nightmare that we experienced that year.

Mother's Bad Hair Day

by Christine Vincent

At 57 years of age, I had just purchased my very first cell phone. I bought the simplest one I could find as this new technology is just beyond my grasp.

However, my daughter Gabby, was excited about me taking my first step into this modern age. She was more than happy to show me how to use my new phone. She was running down the list of what the phone could do when she excitedly explained to me that I could do three-way calling, and that she, Aunt Heather and I could all talk together at once.

While my daughter was explaining this to me, it brought back memories of my childhood. Remember the days of the old party lines, when you shared your phone line with three or more people. This brought back a very funny memory when my mother was waiting for a call from the doctor. Remember those days when you called the doctor and the doctor called you back? Not the receptionist?

There were three people on our party line:

My mother, who was the registered nurse;

Myrtle, the hypochondriac who had every illness in the book and then some; and

Gladis, the neighborhood busybody who had her nose into everyone's business and had a knack for making a mole hill into a mountain.

One morning right after breakfast—I was about 10 years old—I was sitting on the stairs listening to my mother on the phone. She was trying to get hold of the doctor, as my brother, Ted, was sick in bed and Mother had important questions about his medication.

Of course Myrtle and Gladis were on the line with their gossip. It took Mother several tries to butt into the conversation to get them to hang up so the doctor could call her back.

The phone rang; this time it was the doctor when my mother answered. No sooner were they on the line when Myrtle and Gladis got on the line too. Myrtle didn't want to pass up the chance to get free advice for her latest illness, although she usually consulted my mother, the registered nurse. Myrtle now had the real McCoy on the line and began asking questions.

I took the chance to sneak downstairs and peek around the corner. Mother, who was usually a very patient woman, tried several times to politely get Myrtle off the line. She was turning beet-red in the face, and getting so angry that you could see the steam rising from her head. I was just in time to see Mother literally gripping the phone. Then, getting her voice from somewhere deep inside her, out of her mouth came, "Myrtle, shut up. You're not dead yet."

I could hear Myrtle taking a gasp of air, than blasting mother back, "Is that anyway to talk to a dying woman, Jean?" Mother's furious reply was, "The day you're dead, I will be sure to put a lovely bouquet of flowers on your grave. Now, I want to speak to the doctor!" I can just imagine what the doctor was thinking. Next you could hear Myrtle slam her phone down, and Mother got to talk to the doctor. However, keep in mind that Gladis had also been listening to everything on the end of her line as well.

My mother finally hung up after talking to the doctor and everything went back to normal until after lunch. Then our doorbell started ringing. Suddenly we had a parade of neighbours at the door with baked goods, all asking how my brother was, and if it were really true that he was dying.

Mother, realizing that Gladis had just made another mole hill into a mountain, had to explain to everyone what was really going on.

Of course, the last one to ring the door was Gladis herself. Mother, at a loss for words, looked at Gladis who was holding out a cup, asking Mother if she could borrow a cup of sugar. When Mother finally found her voice again, her response was, "I am totally out of sugar, good day." Then, she closed the door in Gladis' face.

But the time my father got home for supper, Mother, who was usually there at the door to greet him with a kiss and a cheerful, "How was your day was at work?" was on the couch in tears.

Looking at me, he asked what was going on. I was trying to explain, at 10 years of age, that Mother had been on the phone with the doctor, Myrtle was dying, the neighbors were at the door and they thought that Mother had said that my brother was dying because Gladis said so.

As I was not making much sense to my dad, he asked me, "Christy, your Mother didn't blow up the kitchen again, did she?" He then asked if my brother, Ted, was hurt, and what Myrtle was doing in our kitchen?

Father was referring to a previous incident during which no one was hurt but which scared the wits out of my mother and me. I guess he was thinking someone got hurt this time. In the previous incident, I was home from school, sick in bed, when I heard a loud boom and my mother screamed in horror from the kitchen. Racing downstairs I found Mother under the kitchen table shaking. As I started to ask my mother what was wrong, something fell on my shoulder. Turning to look at my shoulder, I saw a couple of sliced carrots and pieces of dried paint sitting on my shoulder. Looking up, I saw more carrots and paint stuck to the ceiling. It started to rain more carrots on me. Looking to one side of the kitchen, I saw the pressure cooker lid lying on the floor, and looking to the other side of me, I saw the bottom of the pressure cooker lying on the floor. Poor mother had been cooking carrots in the pressure cooker on the stove when it blew on her. That did make quite a bang that I will never forget. When my dad got home, it was just a simple solution of repainting the kitchen.

I told Dad, "No, Mom didn't blow up the kitchen this time." I was feeling so sorry for Dad as he walked into all the day's confusion as well as into a total communication breakdown. As I wasn't much help in explaining things, he turned his attention to my mother.

Dad said, "Jean darling, what happened today?" Mother started crying even harder and between sobs blurted out how my brother, Ted, was dying because she said so. The neighbors believed her because she was a nurse and Gladis can't mind her own business.

Looking back on it now, Dad must have thought we had totally lost our minds. Even my brother wasn't much help when father asked him what happened. Ted had been asleep through the whole thing upstairs in bed.

However, my dad, being the patient man he was, took my mother's hand and said, "Jean dear, why don't you start from the beginning?" So Mother, wiping away her tears told Dad the whole story. When she finished, she realized she hadn't given Dad a kiss and asked how his day at work was. As she asked him, he replied with, "My day could not possibly compare to the day you just had with all that drama and excitement. In fact, it was an average day at the office; now let's make the rest of this day an enjoyable one. Dear Jean, you put your feet back and rest, I'm cooking dinner tonight." I am sure Dad was thinking about the day my mother had blown up the kitchen and the state mother was in today, he should cook dinner, so we still had our kitchen intact. Today's problem was more than just putting on a new coat of paint. Thanks to my dad, he made the home right side up again.

This was a time when the woman stayed home, cooked and cleaned while the husband went out and worked. The real *Leave It to Beaver* era.

On a parting note from the cell phones with the three-way calling and the social media of today, it's not much different than the party lines of yesteryear. In fact, my daughter Gabby was able to make a six-way call on her cell phone with our friends all on the line at once.

So much for today's social media, Facebook, etc. The good old party line has not died and gone the way of the dinosaurs.

The biggest thing I learned early in life and is true to this day is that gossip and bullying are damaging. If only every generation could put this lesson into practice, and not use technology to further gossip.

I told this story recently to a high school student by telling him this generation uses technology that our generation invented. They will determine if it is good or bad. The next generation will be the guardians of how technology is used, for today and in the future. If properly used there is so much hope for the future.

I can only hope my grandchildren and great grandchildren reap the benefits of what our generation gave to the future.

Never Underestimate the Power of a Desperate Woman

by Ruth Knapp

Raccoons, in the past few years, have become a real menace to our urban society. When my husband and I lived in Barrhaven, a suburb of Ottawa, our house was targeted by these annoying creatures. We fought a losing battle with these clever little beasts for over four years. They resided in our attic.

During the battle period, we actually caught and removed twelve raccoons from the area. Finally, we seemed to be rid of them and we breathed a big sigh of relief. For over a year we were free of those pesky raccoons. Then, one morning about 4 am, I awoke to a rattling outside our bedroom window, only to have my worst fears realized. There, climbing boldly up my husband's ham radio antenna tower, were not one, but two, big, fat, scruffy raccoons! They were already half way up to the roof.

Since I had recently been told that 'coons hate dogs, I threw open the window and began barking. "Bark, Bark, Bark, Bark!!!" Momentarily, our intruders stopped to stare at me, not in the least surprised, but with a look of utter disdain that would have discouraged a less frightened and determined person than myself. When they turned back to continue their climb, undeterred, I began barking even louder, faster and more desperately than before.

At that moment, Bob, my husband, awoke to a sitting position and he exclaimed, "My God, Ruth, what are you doing?" To which I quickly and matter-of-factly replied, "I'm getting rid of the 'coons".

Bob roared, “Don’t be ridiculous! Shut the window. You’ll waken the neighbors. Do you realize what time it is?”

“I don’t really care what time it is or who I waken as long as I get rid of these damn ’coons” was my thoughtful retort. Immediately, I leaned back out the window and resumed my agitated and even more desperate barking: BARK! BARK! BARK! BARK! BARK! BARK! BARK! BARK!

This time the ’coons stood stark still—finally I had their full attention. They looked at me like I was some crazed animal. Within a few seconds, however, they grudgingly began a slow, rung by rung descent and lumbered away through our neighbour’s hedge.

The next evening, I was playing bridge with my neighbor, Myrna, who lived across the street from us, and who owns a Basset hound named, Max. As I was regaling the bridge club with this story, Myrna interrupted me, “Oh, Oh . . . don’t say anything to my husband, Ernie, about this, because at around 4 am he was awakened by Max who had heard a dog barking and Max would not settle down until Ernie took him for a walk!"

Learning Skills

Learning the Foxtrot in Rural Manitoba

by Sylvia Findlay

In the spring of 1948, my eldest brother Bill, then twenty-three, was quite proficient at the two-step polka; however, he needed more expertise if he wished to be cool with the ladies. To succeed, new dance steps had to be learned to expand his bag of tricks. He wondered how he could learn the steps without feeling awkward, practising in public. He settled on a strategy; he decided to order a book on dancing instruction!

The book arrived and the desired fox-trot was demonstrated in narrative and patterns of the dance steps. Holding the book, he tried to follow the dance. It was useless; he could not look at the book and watch his feet at the same time. What to do? Another idea lit up in his brain. He would invite his 18-year-old brother, Sam, to join him.

The brothers found brown paper; drew and cut out several left and right footprints and whipped up a batch of flour and water paste. Needing a venue they agreed the hayloft of the rib-roofed barn would be perfect! It was spring and the animals were out to pasture; the loft was virtually empty until late summer.

Clutching the paper footprints and flour paste they scrambled up the wooden ladder to the loft. Forking the old hay into the corners to clear a dance floor was a dusty itchy task. The next procedure was to arrange the footsteps in the proper pattern. Consulting the book they pasted them to the loft floor. Very good! The lay-out was exactly as indicated on the page.

Next problem, no dance partners; neither was going to be the girl, or dance backwards. They devised an innovative scheme. Pitchforks, tines up and away from the face, gave the illusion of a partner without obscuring the diagram glued to the floor. Grasping the pitch-forks and ready to dance, they encountered still another problem. They had no music! But fortunately Sam was musical and a really good whistler.

Both young men practised the moves as Sam whistled songs such as *Give Me Five Minutes More.* When Sam tired of whistling and dancing simultaneously, a short break was necessary; then back they would go to the pitchforks and brown paper footprints.

Making good progress they agreed to meet in the hayloft each evening. Soon both were good dancers. I was fortunate to gain from their hard earned lessons. Sam, now deceased, taught me to dance and we spent many enjoyable evenings cruising around the Manitoba country side checking out the dance halls.

Bill is 88 now and he still has a passion for dancing. The fox-trot remains a favorite but he also enjoys tangos, the cha cha, English and Viennese waltzes, the French minuet and all types of social dances.

Is it not amazing what can be learned from a book, while partnered with a pitchfork in a barn with a younger brother who could really whistle?

Lessons Learned in a Country Schoolhouse

by Patricia Stockwell

I grew up on a peach farm in a small community called Olinda, near Leamington, Ontario, the Tomato Capital of Canada. Olinda consisted of four corners with the United Church on one corner, the Unitarian on another and the schoolhouse on another. It was a three-room schoolhouse when I went there but when my father was a boy, it had only been one room. He had even had one of the same teachers, Miss Denovan, the principal.

I remember my first grade teacher, Miss Augustine. (There was no such thing as junior and senior kindergarten back in the fifties.) I recall, in particular, the day Miss Augustine handed out pictures of people in different careers for us to colour. "Now, children, these are called professions—all the jobs that people in our community do. Colour them carefully; then we will talk about them," she instructed. I looked at the pictures carefully. Why were all the doctors, police and firefighters men and the secretaries and nurses women? Couldn't a girl be a doctor or even a dentist? I started to colour the pictures, carefully drawing skirts and long hair on the firemen and policemen and pants on the secretaries and nurses.

Miss Augustine came around to look at my work. "Patty, why have you put skirts on the firemen and policemen? Don't you know that girls are not firemen? Girls can be secretaries or nurses or of course, teachers but not firemen. It's too dangerous for girls. Here's a new batch of pictures. Start over," she commanded and continued on to the next student. I was taken aback. What is she talking about? She doesn't know anything. I am not going to be a nurse or a teacher. I am going to be a doctor and go to Africa as a missionary. This was an important lesson for me and the beginning of my feminist leanings.

Later on, in grade eight, I temporarily forgot my feminist views and became boy crazy. I had a crush on a cute, dark-haired boy in my class. One day, my secret love, Larry, brought peppermints to class and passed them out to all his friends when the teacher wasn't looking. Miss Denovan smelled the mints and demanded to know who had them. No one put up a hand. When Miss Denovan turned to the blackboard, Larry wandered down the row of desks and dropped the mints in the side drawer of my desk. Furious that no-one had admitted to having the candy, she began to search desks. I was not worried because I hadn't noticed what Larry had done but when Miss Denovan came to my desk, she found the candies, much to my surprise. "Patty, you lied to me. That's much worse than having candy in class. You will learn a lesson from this. Come with me."

She led me to her office and pulled out the strap. "It's the first time I've ever had to strap a girl but I can't tolerate lying," she said.

I started shaking. "It wasn't me. Someone put them in my desk. I can't tell you who did it but it wasn't me."

"So help me, if you are lying again! Tell me who it was and I'll let you off," she said.

"I can't, Miss Denovan. I really can't"

"In that case, I have no choice. Hold out your hands."

Rubbing my palms together, I returned to the classroom and sat down at my desk, acutely aware of the absolute silence in the room. I didn't cry. I was too angry. Didn't Miss Denovan know that loyalty was more important than always telling the truth—especially loyalty to one that you loved?

I learned many things from those teachers, including algebra and correct grammar, but the more important life lessons have stayed with me after all those years.

Extra Gang Summer

by Earl Lytle

The two of us (Earl and Don) had just graduated from high school and had found labouring jobs for the summer with the Canadian Pacific Railway. We left early one June morning and drove with Don's father to join the "Extra Gang" at the hamlet of Wilkinson, Ontario. Wilkinson consisted of three houses as well as a small CPR yard. Don's father was the assistant foreman of the gang and he provided excellent advice to us recruits such as which gang members to avoid.

The extra gang was formed each summer by the CPR. It consisted of about 40 unskilled labourers. Its purpose was to fill in on the many additional jobs that took place on the railway during this period.

It was summer of 1957 and the pay was 80 cents an hour for a 10 hour day. After several weeks of commuting, we started to live with the gang and we paid for our room and board. Although bunks were available in a railway sleeping car, Don and I were lucky, as we stayed in a modified caboose with two young lads from Quebec. Both Dan and Charlie could communicate in both French and English, while Sick Turkey and I were unilingual but not in the same tongue.

One of our first jobs was "tamping tracks". This involved applying extra gravel to the railway bed. The gravel was brought to the site in hopper cars. These cars had doors in the bottom which were opened at the top to let the gravel out as the train moved slowly forward. Most of the gang followed the train tamping the gravel into the spaces where it was required.

We were assigned to the top of the cars where we insured that the gravel kept flowing. There were two dangers; the first was never to be in the center of the car when the doors were open, to avoid being smothered. The other was to be alert at the end of the load if you were shovelling down in the hopper. It was considered good fun for those on top to send large stones down the shoot. If such was the case, the rumbling of the fast descending stones was a signal to move fast to avoid being hit. It was common to look up after such an occurrence to see the "POW" with a satisfied grin on his face looking down.

We had nicknamed him "POW" as he wore a German army cap, and it was not too long before this, that the survivors of Stalingrad were released from Russian prison camps.

During the summer, several ex-cons recently released from Dorchester prison joined the gang. Apparently it was a condition of their parole that they work on the gang. They wore street clothes and shoes and were not enthusiastic workers. We avoided them as much as possible and lucky for us, they headed for the hills when they received their first paycheck, if not before.

The two recent Italian immigrants with us were enthusiastic workers and normally did more than their share. However they left the gang at the first opportunity they had, after learning that there were jobs paying 90 cents an hour shovelling sand.

Mid-summer also saw the arrival of a contingent of workers from the streets of Toronto. Martel was an older educated individual who after hearing that I planned to join the army at the end of the summer strongly advised against it, based on his previous experience with such an organization. One individual from Toronto stood out from all the others for his wildness. Keep in mind that the others from Toronto were not tame in any respect. This individual was dubbed "Black Irish".

Black Irish were very rough looking types, who sported a bowler hat. On the two weekends he stayed with the gang he got into trouble, both times involving alcohol. The first incident got him a warning. While bathing in a tub and singing a playful tune, a passenger train approached on the main line. At this point he stood up, naked, wearing his bowler hat and waved at the passing train with a wine bottle held firmly in the other hand. This episode showed his comedic side, while the next showed a more violent disposition.

The next weekend, which proved to be his last with the CPR, the incident was serious. While under the influence he staggered into town and jumped through a plate glass window attempting to reach the woman of his dreams. He made it back to the sleeping car bleeding quite badly. In an attempt to staunch the flow of blood he used "Black Bob's" sheets. He was last seen heading down the track wrapped in the sheets. Black Bob was the cook, and was not impressed when he heard about the fate of his bedding.

"Lining Bar" was a solid hard worker; however he lacked a sense of humor and had the unique habit of hitting himself in the teeth when under stress. He commuted to the job in a fairly new large gas guzzling car. Big Leo from Quebec always referred to him as Lining Bar and his g_ _ d_ _ _ _ _ _ big car. Lining Bar failed to appreciate this add-on to his name.

Big Leo was not only massive but was a jovial sort, always ready for some new capers. On one occasion a muscular engineer was joking with some of the gang members during a break, and he and Leo got into a shoving match. In no time they were thrashing on the ground and both rolled swiftly down the very steep embankment wrapped together as one. At the bottom they shook hands and sheepishly scrambled up the hill, covered in dirt, and a few new bruises.

Several of the gang were subsistence farmers who worked at summer jobs to earn enough unemployment credits to keep money coming in for the winter months. They spoke of sitting close to a wood stove during the months of February and January.

Mac was an overweight older worker who was unable to keep up to the rest of the workers and was finally given the task of staying behind and cleaning up the sleeping cars. Mac really enjoyed chewing tobacco and invariably had a large bulge in his right cheek. This proved his undoing when one day he swallowed a large wad of it and was rushed to the hospital. He never returned to the job.

The food was good although you had to develop a good boarding house reach in order to get your share of the coveted fried eggs in the morning and the delicious pies in the evening. While on the job we all shared the same dipper when quenching our thirst from the large keg of water. On the job bathroom equipment consisted of a shovel and a walk to the nearest bush.

One of the major jobs the gang participated in was laying new tracks. My job was a snap. At every tie I had to drop off several wooden dowels and, sometimes, when the foreman wasn't around I could hitch a ride on a proceeding cart, which allowed me to sit down on the job. When I explained the soft touch to Dan at days-end he shook his head in dismay at the unfairness in the world. He had been assigned one of the toughest jobs. He spent an agonizing day, bent over, feeding spikes with a holder to a huge, noisy machine which hammered them in place. He was not a very happy camper to say the least.

At the end of August we advised the boss and the timekeeper that we were quitting. The boss was named Manion and he was respected by all. I remember the time he took me off the dangerous job of unloading rails because I was too inexperienced.

Thus ended our eye-opening career with the Extra Gang. Shortly thereafter Don entered teachers college while I joined the army.

A Life Changing Experience

by Skip Gillham

It was the summer of 1963. I had just graduated with a B.A. in history from Victoria College, University of Toronto, and decided to pursue a second bachelor degree. A friend of my brother-in-law had made me aware of a one-year Physical Education course at McMaster University designed for university graduates and, as I loved sports and was thinking of a career in teaching, this seemed like a good fit.

But I had been living very economically at home in Toronto, able to pay for my tuition with a summer job and had run a mid-week gym program for Central Neighbourhood House in Toronto to cover my spending money. But living in Hamilton, with no mid-week job, meant I needed a better salary for the summer.

I had often thought about working on a lake boat. When my mother had been very sick in the 1940s, my father often got me out of the house by going to High Park to feed the animals and then see what was tied up in Toronto harbour. He kept a list of the ships that we saw. These outings were a regular occurrence for about two years until my mother succumbed to her illness and our routine changed.

My interest in the ships remained and it was now time to pursue the thought of working on a laker to further my education. I applied to several tanker fleets as they were generally independent and looked favourably at university students. This enabled their regular sailors to get a bit of a break. Early in May, I got a call from Lakeland Tankers to join the Lubrolake in the Welland Canal and it was the beginning of an adventure that I will never forget.

I was hired on as an "oiler" and our ship's engine room was mainly crewed by sailors who hailed from Maritime Canada. This would be home for this recent un-mechanical Arts graduate. The officers and crew on the forward part of the ship were from Quebec and most hailed from the same small town. They spoke French as their mother-tongue and it gave me an opportunity to practice my five years of high school French. Fortunately for me, they also communicated very well in English.

I climbed aboard in the early morning hours of May 13, 1963, as we were headed downbound in the Welland Canal. On board was a cargo of calcium chloride that had been loaded at Ludington, MI for delivery to Prescott, ON. On arrival at the latter port, I was expected to go through the same "Customs check" as the others even though I had joined in Ontario. All went well.

After unloading we proceeded to Montreal. It was my first visit to Quebec and to see it first from the vantage point of the St. Lawrence was a memory I will never forget. The harbour was busy with lakers and ocean going ships scurrying around or at the docks. I saw aging Liberty ships, veterans of World War Two, small and large freighters, and the most modern of the Seaway-sized lake ships. I remember that one, the Black Bay, passed us later on the St. Lawrence like we were standing still.

We loaded at Pointe-aux-Trembles overnight and come morning we were underway east bound to the Saguenay River port of Chicoutimi. I spent the non-working hours on deck watching the sights. We passed Trois Riveries, Quebec City, saw the Plains of Abraham, the magnificent Chateau Frontenac Hotel overlooking the river and the busy shipyard on the south shore at Lauzon. I noticed that the farms along the river were all narrow and stretched back inland from the river just like the school textbooks had described our earliest settlers living under the Seigneurial System.

The St. Lawrence widened as we headed east and once we reached the Saguenay River, we turned north. I had never seen anything like the steep granite cliffs that rose straight up for hundreds of feet out of the water. Cape Trinity and Cape Eternity were unforgettable. I was disappointed, however, when we arrived off Chicoutimi and unloaded via a pipeline connection while anchored in the river. I had been hoping to go ashore.

During the summer we repeated the trip several times and I did get to walk the hilly streets of the town. That was as far east as we ventured but our ship often loaded at Montreal for delivery to Morrisburg, Kingston, Cobourg, Oshawa and Toronto. I settled into the routine and enjoyed the work with the friendly crew who, despite our different cultural and language backgrounds, all got along very well.

I was therefore very surprised when, during a stop to unload in a Quebec port, a local resident came down to the dock to yell some things that were not in my French-English dictionary and then spit several times at our Canadian Ensign flag flying on the stern. It was my first exposure to the strong feelings among some who clearly favoured separation from Canada.

My time slot was 8:00 am to 12 noon and 8:00 pm to midnight. One evening, after coming off our shift, I made a sandwich and joined the Third Engineer on the back deck as we headed upbound in the St. Lawrence. We watched a saltwater ship glide by headed for the sea and it was recognized, from the stack emblem, as a member of the Head Line.

We awoke in the morning to find the Lubrolake at anchor in the thickest fog I had ever experienced. There was a sombre mood in the galley. There I learned that there was an overnight collision a few miles to our east that sank the ore ship Tritonica with the loss of 33 lives. The second ship involved was the Roonagh Head of the Head Line. To this day I wondered if it was the freighter we had seen only hours before the fatal collision.

By the end of July, I thought I had enough money to finance one more year of school so I left the ship for some time in Muskoka before resuming my education. While I had joined the ship to pay for that education, I found that my summer aboard provided an eye opening education of its own on the geography, history and politics of our country.

I headed to McMaster for what proved to be my most enjoyable and most successful year of school. It was my final preparation for a wonderful career as a high school teacher in Waterford and Beamsville. I taught for 33 years and, after retirement, returned to coach track and field for an additional ten years before hanging up my whistle for the last time. I paid for this career opportunity by working on the lakes and left school with no debts thanks to that memorable summer.

The Clove Hitch Knot

by Caroline O'Leary-Hartwick

The day was stormy as I watched my grandfather. With his net piled beside him he sat at the kitchen window that overlooked the sea. This was his spot to do his work. Even on this stormy day the window gave him enough light to do his work. A cozy fire was roaring in the wood stove with a pot of tea perking on the side. The house had a combined smell of sea salt and tar from the nets, wood smoke from the stove, and cooking odours, as my grandmother was always cooking.

I was always impressed by how quickly his hands moved. He seldom wasted movements. With swift precision he moved the net needle in and out to make the clove hitch knot that was required to mend his net using the spacer to gauge the amount of twine to leave between each knot. I would stand beside him for a long time admiring his ability. Every once in a while he would look up and observe the sea and comment on the waves or the wind.

One day as I watched him threading his needle with twine, and he asked, "Would you like to learn how?" I nodded, bobbing my head up and down excitedly. He smiled, his one toothed grin, pleased. He sat me on his lap, and with his arms encircling me proceeded to first teach me how to thread the net needle. My fingers were short and not as nibble as his and it took me quite a while to get the hang of the in and out of the twine and turn and in and out again until the net needle was full of twine. That was the beginning of learning his craft. He showed me how to use the spacer so all the net holes would be the same size and finally to make the clove hitch knot, I would practice with him for a long time biting my tongue in contrition. He was always patient with me and seldom criticized, but just kept me repeating each step til I had accomplished it.

The memories of these times with my grandfather are very special to me; I can still feel the roughness of his flannel work shirt, and his special smell of salt, soap and smoke surrounding me. I can feel the calmness and praise of encouragement in his voice, with gentle touch of leathery hand as he taught me. I know it made me want to please him.

Rug Hooking

by Margaret Amyotte

It's 1948; Dad had purchased a three-bedroom log house, on the outskirts of Kirkland Lake, a Northern Ontario town. Even without the city's commodities, it was quite comfortable. The Aladdin lamp provided us with almost as much light as electricity.

My fondest recollection was of those hundred pound burlap potato bags. Even in those days, before and after the war, recycling was a way of life. Mom washed the bags, and then they were used to make floor mats, or rugs. Nothing potentially reusable was ever thrown away.

In those days, money was a rarity, and coming from a family of seven children, meant we had to find ways to supplement ways to survive. Our mother especially had a rare gift for this. During those long winter months, with only a battery operated radio to listen to, our parents had to be resourceful, and devise ways to keep us occupied. Dad, being very artistic, had designed the older children each a crochet hook, carved out of wood, with a small nail inserted in it. The tip was filed into a hook, a unique one to fit our hands. I always kept mine as a souvenir. In fact, it has become a piece of conversation over the years.

Then the clean potato bag was cut in half. Dad would then, with a piece of chalk, draw scenery on it. Mom would help one of us cut different colors of remnants into quarter-inch strips.

The bag was then attached on a wooden frame, which Dad had

also fabricated. Every capable child was given a task. Some would separate different coloured strips of cloth, and hand them to us. Then Dad and a couple of others hooked them to fit the scenery. We would hold the strip under the bag with our left hand and with the other pull it through the hook, in each little hole of the bag, a finesse that we quickly learned to manoeuvre.

This was done in the evening by the Aladdin lamp, after our homework and chores were done, and during the weekend. Oddly enough, we enjoyed and looked forward to this hobby, and challenge. It took a couple of weeks to make it into a work of art. Once completed, Mom proudly displayed it in our living room. By the end of the winter, we had made a total of four.

Of course, it wasn't all work, we would listen to the radio or sing along with the gramophone, that one of the younger children would volunteer to crank.

Some of our visitors were fascinated by the intricacies of the work of the mats, and some would even offer to buy them. Mom was a great home decorator, placing everything in its convenient and most appealing place, along with flowers that we had also made out of tissue paper.

This and many other things our parents invented to keep us occupied during those long winter months. It also kept our family working together.

These are some of my favorite memories. Frankly, I would not change these memories for all the money in the world.

Oh, How Things Have Changed

The Ice Man

by Colleen McRae

When my mind travels back to the cherished time of my childhood, my heart experiences the joy of a ten-year-old in the bosom of a summer filled with laughter, friends and innocence.

Yes, life was wonderful.

Our safe and loving home with my mother, sister and grandmother was across from our big, beautiful Riverdale Park which encompassed most of the other side of Broadview Avenue in east Toronto. A short walk through the park, across the wooden bridge over the Don River which was full of ducks and clear water brought us to the Riverdale Zoo, which became a Sunday excursion each week, while still in our best church clothes. The zoo was my sister's and my treat for behaving during the service. And it was free.

Yes, life was wonderful.

Roller skates were my mode of transport, as we could not afford bicycles. I loved to put the big tightening key on a ribbon around my neck and watch it dangle as I skated blissfully along the pavement. How important I thought I was to have a key of my own, and not yet in my teens. When I skated in my neighbourhood, I owned the world and everything in it. I truly belonged.

Summer was magical on Broadview Avenue. On Tuesdays, we children would follow the Rags and Bone Man in his wagon calling out, "Rags and Bones." This made us feel that we were part of his parade; the noise of our skates against the pavement accompanied his rash solo voice.

My favourite day in the summer was Wednesday, for on that day each week the Ice Man came. My friends and I would wait expectantly at the corner of Broadview and Withrow Avenue, and we could hear his old, noisy truck coming towards us long before it appeared. Gleefully, we would race toward the back of his truck and skate along behind him, some braver ones hanging on to it to get a free skate. He had his route and we knew where it was. When he alit from his truck and walked toward the back where stacks of ice blocks were stored, he would smile and pretend to be surprised to see a little group of roller skaters behind the truck. Then he would chip some ice from the block before he put it in a burlap wrap and say, "A little too much ice on this one I think." We would look at each other beaming with excitement. Once the Ice Man left to make his delivery, our plan would commence. As fast as we could, we would grab the little icicles thinking we had really put it over on him, and skate off with our loot, happily sucking the melting ice before it was gone.

Yes, life was wonderful.

Today, whenever I see an icicle perched precariously on an eave or a tree branch, my heart warms immediately to the softness of my 1951 summer days reflecting the prism the icicle represented to a ten-year-old, in roller skates, owning her own world, and everything in it. Now, as a senior, I can still attest that, even though the Ice Man never more cometh,

Yes, life is still wonderful.

Bicycles Then and Now

by Kevin Delaney

To be in the cockpit of a bipane fighter or leading the pack while roaring around a dirt track on your motor bike were grand things to do as a 10-year-old boy in small city Ontario in the fifties. Playing out of doors when the weather was good during those endless days of summer vacation was your amusement. No video games, TV barely started, day time programing involved soap commercials and was meant for your mother. Kid programs would not be on the tube until just before supper. At this moment in time kids were meant to be out of doors. In the summer to keep your 10-year-old self amused you needed three things, friends, bikes and imagination.

You would find yourself racing off down the side streets of your city on your imaginary motor cycle.

Modifying the sound of your bike with a clothes peg and unwanted hockey or baseball cards was the trick. Simply bend the card around the fork, clip it with the peg and let the exposed end flap against the spokes as you sped down the street. The more cards you could clamp on to the front and back forks the louder the sound.

It was great fun until your mother noticed the clothes peg count was low and made you give all but one or two back. Then it was off again, working your way through town trying to get to the edge of the river to look for crayfish, tadpoles and minnows. Once you tired of that it was time to saddle up on your imaginary horse and head off to the corner store for supplies. Once well supplied, you and your posse then headed to the woods by the railway tracks.

Having arrived at the woods near the tracks you needed to hide your imaginary horses and move carefully through the woods looking for the camps of Indians or robbers that were sure to be planning to attack the trains as they rolled by. With the long abandoned camps found there was nothing else to do but eat your recently purchased supplies and discuss your next move. It was getting hot so the best thing would be to spend the afternoon at the community swimming hole otherwise known as the municipal pool. Peddle home quick, secure the quarter needed for both admission and the locker. Your swim suit on, a towel tucked under your arm, remounted on the bike and off to the agreed intersection where you would all meet a ride together to the pool.

This cycle would be repeated over and over again throughout the summer. In your imagination the bike would be a horse, plane, motorcycle or race car. The adventure would be based on what Saturday afternoon matinée was seen or going to be seen. Finally the days of vacation would draw to a close. The bike would revert to your transportation to and from school. At school, dismounting you walked your bike over to the rack hung it up by the handle bars next to your friends alongside hundreds of other bikes. Heading off to find friends in the yard. Finally the too-cool days of autumn would signal the end of the seasons of the bike. The bike was now stored in the shed to await the liberty and freedom of spring.

The Clothes Line

by Linda Wilson

Looking back, to a world I perceive as a gentler, easier place, I now marvel at how many of the things I took for granted as a child have disappeared. My children have no recollection of crank telephones or rain barrels or the haymows I loved at my Grammie Kirk's farm in rural Nova Scotia. They never got to explore dusty attics searching for long-forgotten treasures, or smelly chicken coops gathering fresh-laid eggs. Today's children are more likely to visit Grammie at her high-rise condo, when she can fit them in between trips to Florida, and lunch at the golf club.

One of the homeliest yet most important tools of past generations was the lowly clothesline. Be it a simple rope strung between two poles and propped up with a stick to keep its burden of clean wet sheets from dragging on the ground, or a fancy mechanized pulley system that took ones dainties sailing across the yard, every home boasted one of its own. And there was a ritual tied to this line that was almost sacred . . . Monday was laundry day. The bed sheets were changed and the family's dirty clothes rounded up and subjected to a good scrubbing in the wringer washer, with lots of hot water and strong lye soap. No doubt there were prayers offered on Sunday night for Divine intervention in regards to the next day's weather forecast.

In communities where homes were close enough for the neighbors to scrutinize each others activities, there was an unspoken competition. The most diligent got their chores started at the crack of dawn. As soon as the last child was out the door to school, the race was on to get the laundry on the line. Reputations rose and fell with the clothesline, and form was just as important as speed. No housewife worth her salt would think of deviating from the accepted rules . . . first the sheets, next the towels, in order of size and then the personal whites, otherwise known as unmentionables. How innocent were we that the mere sight of old ladies' bloomers or a pair of trap-door long johns would send us children into fits of laughter! The second string was devoted to colours: shirts, trousers and socks. In large families, the whole day was consumed with this monumental task.

My most vivid memory concerning a clothesline involves an up close and personal encounter. My grandmother had, besides her heavy duty day line out the back door, off the "summer kitchen", a shorter line around the front of the farmhouse, where she usually had a few small pieces such as dish towels drying. Her little rocking chair was by the window overlooking that very spot.

I am inclined to think now, that she used that line as a kind of weather indicator. She could assess the direction and speed of the wind by how hard and which way her towels were blowing. For some reason this line was actually a thin length of wire, and given that it was used for light duty only, it did not need to be very thick. Therein lay the problem.

On a beautiful summer day, I went racing around the corner of the house, no doubt on some important mission, and at full tilt into that clothesline. It struck me right across the bridge of my nose. Given the tensile strength inherent in stainless steel wire, of course it did not break. I was brought up short, and then smacked backwards, slamming my head on the ground. I do not know how long I lay there, but eventually I came to and was ushered into the house. Some sympathy was no doubt proffered, but in this no-nonsense Scots

Presbyterian family, it would have been liberally accompanied by advice on the foolishness of children and an often repeated: "Are you trying to kill yourself?" from my (childless) Uncle Aubrey. To this day I carry a faint scar from this mishap. I call it my life line.

The Green Jug

by Ida May Gardiner

The jug sat inside a large white bowl on the top of Mom and Dad's dresser. Although they say the Irish can see 40 shades of the stuff, the jug was never described as anything other than green. There might have been some sort of charming design on it, maybe some raised flowers, but that was never remarked upon. It came from the Warren family farm and Mother loved it dearly. We were allowed to handle it rarely, but it was used liberally.

During our summers at the cottage, the only source of water for bathing came from the lake. Most of the time we were handed a bar of hard, yellow Sunlight soap, pointed in the direction of the water and told to "go get washed", but once a week Mother bravely undertook the marathon of hair washing.

The battered aluminium kettle was filled to the brim with lake water and set on the stove to boil. Once steam was fleeing into the air and water jumping out from underneath the ill-fitting lid, it was time to begin. Mother, and only Mother, was responsible for alternating between pouring in boiling hot water and cold lake water into the green jug until a temperature balance was achieved. In this manner, the jug remained crack free.

We would each line up and take our turn with our heads hung over the kitchen sink. Mother would pour a little water over your head and then add shampoo and scrub like the dickens. Then more water would be poured all over your head. There was no pleasure to be found in the activity but my sister, Cathy, and I seemed to tolerate the procedure fairly well. Our brother Warren, however, would not.

Warren would scream: "Too hot! Too hot!" He would also jump away from the sink. It didn't matter what the temperature actually was it was always the same. Water would fly all over the counter tops and all over the floor.

Arguments would ensue and eventually he would get back up to the sink. Then the Soap was added.

"My eyes!! My eyes!!" he would holler. "There's soap in my eyes!!" Again he would jump away. More arguments, more coaxing and more cajoling brought him back to the sink. There was a lively debate over how hard Mother was scrubbing or not scrubbing but eventually, a round of rinsing would bring the whole thing to an end.

After the mess was cleaned up and the kitchen back in order Mother re-fired the kettle and did her own hair. I don't ever recall Dad having to undergo this water-boarding technique.

Mother would then fill up her jug with warm water and retire to her bedroom where she had her bowl waiting. She would perform her "sponge-bath" in private and emerge in her housecoat ready to relax. The bowl was emptied into the sink, dried and placed on her dresser and the green jug lovingly returned to the nest once more.

The Green Jug survived our generation and is now in the care of my mother's great nephew.

One Long Two Short

by Linda Wilson

In the farmhouses along the Florida Road, the kitchen was the place to be. With its roaring wood stove and comfy couch for after supper lounging, my Grammie Kirk's kitchen was no exception. It was a large rectangular room with a linoleum floor, worn in places by the passing feet of 11 children and their parents, and later their spouses and their children. Tucked into a corner between the stove and a built- in desk/ cupboard was a plain little wooden chair. I never saw anyone actually sitting there, as Grammies rocking chair was directly in front of this arrangement, right by the window. But it became my favourite spot from which to observe the goings on of this large and noisy family.

On the wall above the desk hung an object of great fascination to all of us grandchildren . . . Grammies telephone. It wasn't a boring little black machine like we all had at home, but a large wooden box with a handle for cranking on the side. There was a little funnel shaped opening you spoke into (or shouted into, depending on how far away the person you were speaking to was located) , and a receiver you held up to your ear, which was attached to the box by a rather short wire. In those days everyone out in the country had what was called a party line, meaning that as many as five households or 'parties' shared one line.

Each family had its own distinctive ring pattern, such as one long ring followed by two short rings. And of course everyone knew their neighbour's ring. Chances were that if you lifted the receiver at random, you would hear someone speaking. If you were very quiet, and there was nobody in the kitchen to catch you, you could hear Mrs. Flanagan ordering her groceries, or Bertha Cooper talking to her daughter Bunny down the road. Sometimes it was hard not to make any noise, especially when my cousin Gayle and I were together and the person on the line would say "Is there someone there? Did you hear that Winnie? I think somebody's listening in." in an indignant voice. We would be consumed by fits of giggles, and have to hang up.

Of course listening in was an illicit pleasure, and we were in big trouble if we got caught. But we knew that the grownups did it too. Sometimes we overheard hushed discussions about various happenings along the road, that were attributed to "so-and-so" said this or that. I don't ever remember Grammie being involved in these conversations. She just sat in her rocker and knitted, with a little smile playing on her lips. In fact, I don't remember her talking much at all. Perhaps she had used up all her words raising those eleven children.

One occasion I remember well was a call from my Aunt Greta and her husband Carl when they were stationed in Longuyon, France with the Air Force. It may have been Grammie's birthday, as calls were not made frivolously in those days. Every one up and down the line knew the call was coming. How they knew this I don't know, but when the call came there were so many clicks on the line, Grammie could hardly hear a thing.

We children were sure it was because the power that carried the words across the wires seeped out of every telephone that was lifted off its hook. At any rate Grammie was thrilled with the call, and not even annoyed at all the eavesdropping that day—after all the neighbours would be marveling about how Clara Kirk's youngest daughter had, "called her mother all the way from overseas. Just imagine!"

I believe the crank style telephones were phased out in the mid 1960s, replaced by shiny black plastic beauties and private lines. Gone too were the local operators who were always willing to have a little chat with you when you sought their help in placing a call. It was the end of another era in rural Nova Scotia.

Annie Oakley Rides Again

by Patricia Stockwell

My best Christmas ever was the year I turned ten. I got the two things I had wished for most in the whole world—my Mickey Mouse ears and my Annie Oakley holster and cap gun. The Mickey Mouse ears were cool but I was particularly in awe of the holster and cap gun. The holster was tan leather decorated with brown fringe and a black outline of a cowgirl riding a bucking bronco all the while twirling a lasso over her head—Annie Oakley herself.

Annie Oakley was my heroine along with Annette Funicello on the Mickey Mouse Clubhouse. I never imagined that a girl could out-ride, out-shoot and out-talk the cowboys. After all, I was a child of the 50s when a woman wouldn't dare out-talk a man, let alone out-ride and out-shoot one.

Every day at 4 pm after school, I would put on my Mousketeer ears, turn on the Phillips black-and-white TV and pretend that I was Annette Funicello dancing with Bobby Burgess. Then, still wearing my Mousketeer headgear, I would strap on my holster and gun and settle down to watch the Annie Oakley show. When Annie chased the bad guys, I hid behind my Dad's Lazyboy and fired off shots at the bandits. I loved the sound of the caps exploding just like those little red firecrackers we lit on July 1. The smell of the acrid smoke filled my nostrils and the thrill of danger filled my heart. I was right there along with Annie, pursuing justice and righting the wrongs of the world.

Years later, as an adult, I found myself fighting the bad guys in real life and the bad guys in my psyche. Thanks to Annie, I learned to out-ride, out-shoot and out-talk those bad guys, just like Annie Oakley herself.

Pioneer Camp

by Richard Standish

Long before the days of child coddling and political correctness, my older brother Ed and I went to teen camp at Pioneer Camp, outside of Port Sydney, Ontario for one week in August 1954. Ed had heard about the camp through Inter-varsity Christian Fellowship meetings at High School. Very quickly I knew I didn't want to be a camper but I liked the camp itself, the atmosphere and the new friends I met.

The next summer Ed had acquired a '35 Plymouth that burned a quart of oil every 50 miles. We headed out for pre-camp Easter weekend as volunteer workers and went every weekend until camp opening in June. Then we became part of the maintenance staff and worked there every summer until 1962. The director, who was called Cobber because he came from Australia, was our boss but our immediate supervisor was an old guy named Wainwright and we called him Drainpipe. He smoked, which was a sin at the seriously religious camp, but even Cobber couldn't stop him. Drainpipe just said it kept the mosquitoes and black flies away.

We were 14 and were allowed and expected to do just about everything except sin. For example we used industrial-sized equipment with no training, which would never be allowed today. We moved whole buildings, built underwater cribs to hold the docks using a makeshift scuba diving mask which had an air compressor stuck in a hole so we could breathe. We graded roads, dug ditches, loaded 10-ton trucks with gravel using only hand shovels, maintained a team of horses for the covered wagon rides, learned to use a cement mixer and poured a 2ft wide x 6ft high x 30ft long concrete wall, which stands to this day, to hold back an eroding embankment that had a huge building on top of it, and cleaned out septic tanks with no idea about toxic gases.

With my two best friends Ted and Skip it was always a race to see who could complete the task the fastest. For example we were digging 5ft deep post holes for a hydro line in the bush so there were roots and stones and boulders to remove and with each hole we competed for time. We had to figure out how to dynamite stumps without getting killed, hand drill holes in rocks in the road to be dynamited, carry a full butchered quarter of beef into the huge refrigerators to be slaughtered for the three camps, boys, girls, and junior. Every job was a wonderful race. This lasted from 1954–62 and as we got older we did bigger and more dangerous jobs.

My reward for all this was that I got rescued from the Bible study and praying circle before bed because I was so tired I fell asleep soon after supper. Again in the morning, before religious activities started, I would be rescued again by a maintenance man calling for me to help and I loved it!

We had very little supervision and no concern for safety. There was never a question of "what if". Someone would hand you an industrial sized Dewalt radial saw and say go and cut that board out of the girls bathroom. We felt privileged because they believed we could do whatever was asked. At one point in 1961 Ted, Skip and I went west on a road trip and stopped at another Pioneer Camp in Lake of the Woods. We had to be canoed into the camp by an Aboriginal guide. The camp directors wanted a 1000-gallon tank moved to a new location. They said that we had to drain the tank but the three of us said that we would move it full. We did it and left the next day successful because of our training at Pioneer Camp. It was amazing that no one was killed!

That doesn't mean there weren't accidents. There was a guy from Germany and his favorite song was Be My Tedzzy Bear and he wore leiderhosen. We were painting creasote on wood siding and it splashed all over him because he wasn't a careful painter. It burnt his skin badly and he was in pain for days after. Another time we were pouring a concrete wall and one of the rookie workers said he could stop the gas-driven cement mixer by grabbing the pulley. Not so. he got his hands ripped by the pulley and off to the infirmary he went! One day, six of us were loading gravel on a three-ton truck by hand, sweating like horses all day. It was an extremely hot day. At 8:00 pm I was feeling sick to my stomach and went to the infirmary. The nurse thought that I had appendicitis and she got the doctor to come and look at me. By that time all of my muscles had cramped in my arms and legs and my tongue had swollen so much that I couldn't talk. The doctor had spent time in very hot countries and recognized my condition as complete dehydration. He made me drink warm salt water until my muscles relaxed. In four days I was back to normal and back on the front lines.

Another episode that shows the lack of safety protocol in those days was that we had to put a fire out at the dump. We had an airplane fuel tank filled with water and back packs filled with water from the tank. It was midnight and pitch black. We put the fire out and then we were ordered back to camp. The senior staff stayed to make sure the fire was out. Left to find our way back to camp, approximately a mile on a twisty gravel road, we marched six abreast and when one end person felt he was going off the road then we would move the whole line the other way. That continued until we finally got back to camp.

This year in 2014 we went to the 50th Anniversary of Pioneer Camp in Port Sydney. It was wonderful to remember all the years that I had shared with my friends Ted and Skip in our cabin called TEDICKIP. We are so happy to still be friends after 50 years and we still keep in touch now in our 70s. What a wonderful gift!

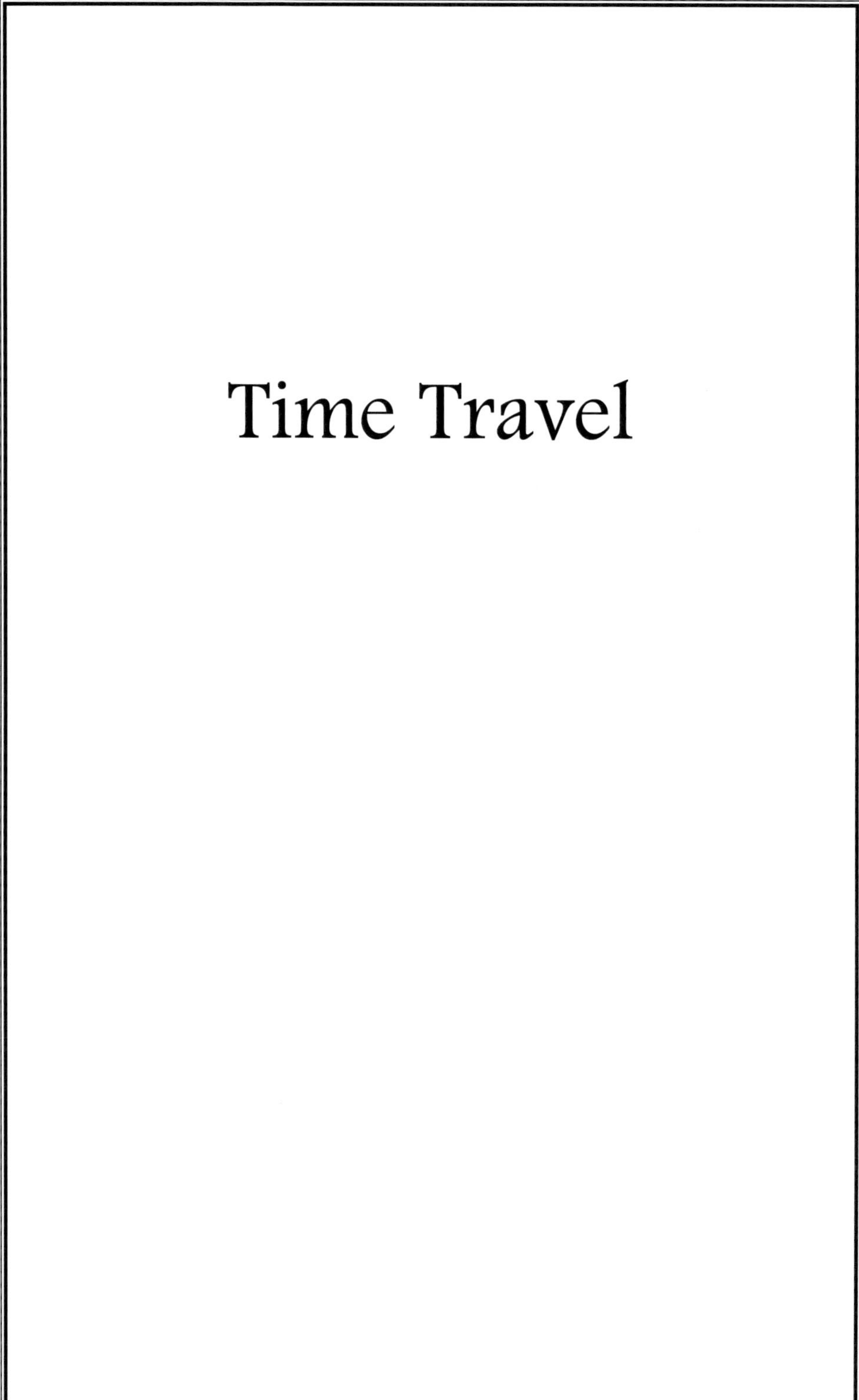

Time Travel

Ottawa

by Janet Beers

My relationship with this glorious city has been a roller coaster ride for the last 64 years. My life began in Halifax in January of 1944 when my mother rushed pregnant from Huntingville, PQ to NS to allow my father to see me before he shipped out to serve in WWII. He actually went AWOL to see me and then ended up in the brig. Suffice to say my life has never been boring. As with many Canadian veterans my Dad got to finish school on the DVA plan and then landed a job with Boy Scouts Canada here in Ottawa. By that time I was in Grade One and settled into a new school with new friends in what was then Eastview with my parents and my three-year-old brother. Looking back now I certainly had a great deal of freedom as I walked to school alone along the canal and up Montreal Road. I also went to afternoon matinees at the local theatre on Montreal Road with friends and once ran away to the circus at the local park—I have always loved carnies!

Just when I had a handle on my new life my parents bought a house in the west end of Ottawa in a new subdivision. We were the first house on the street and directly across the road was the Experimental Farm land. As I grew, year by year, more houses arrived and my life was full of family (including eventually three younger brothers), friends, school, pick up baseball games, music lessons, ice skating on the rink that Dad built on our side lawn every winter and cross country skiing at the Mackenzie King estate.

My mum was a stay at home mum and whenever we got home we called out "Mum" and always got an answer. Dad played guitar and mouth organ and sang to us before bed. Our holidays were accompanying Dad to Scout Jamborees across eastern Canada. Most of the adult entertainment, because nobody had much money, were house parties right in our neighborhood with lots of eating and dancing and the children were included or put to bed in one house with an older child babysitting, lots of chaos as I'm sure you can imagine.

By the time I was in Grade Five we had a gang of girl friends who went everywhere together. We were never in the house except to eat or sleep. The only rule was that you had to be home for supper and then back in after supper in time for bed. Because we had freedom to roam at will my dad would whistle his great loud whistle and if we weren't back in 10 minutes we were grounded. As we got older we learned to read the sky and start home so we'd be in range and then of course it taught us to run! My father was always great with the threats. His famous one for grounding was that you are grounded for the rest of your life or until I lose interest. Fortunately he had a reasonably short attention span. Some parents who couldn't whistle used bells or various sirens. One of our yearly initiations, to prove that we weren't chicken, was to wade through a huge discarded culvert beside the railroad tracks which eventually became the Ottawa Queensway. One year there was a dead cow in it and we still all waded through. There were also pools beside the tracks where we went swimming, well actually skinny dipping, until one of our parents found out and put an end to that as there was a polio scare that summer.

The boys our age had a similar gang and by Grade Six we combined forces to build a fort with only an underground entrance. One of the boys was a HAM radio guy so we got to talk to people from all over the world.

Flash forward to teenage years. The boys have cars, and anyone can get one on the road for $50.00. In the beginning it was wonderful!

We still had very little supervision except that we were now becoming aware of the insidious net of children-checking that our parents had set up while we were asleep at the switch. It turned out that there was nowhere that I could go where someone of this network wouldn't see me and without the Internet or Facebook—God they were brilliant!

"OTTAWA THE BORING!" said every teenager but guess what? We figured out that Hull was just across the bridge and now we had wheels!

Oddly enough, guided by our parents, we discovered that Ottawa wasn't boring. It was next door to some of the most famous stars of the time playing venues we could afford to go to and learn something new.

Jump ahead to my adult years. After wanting to escape from boring Ottawa I found the man I loved and he worked in Ottawa. I almost ran but guess what this was, and still is, the most beautiful place to bring up a family. We moved out to Kanata, the new suburban idea created by the brain of Bill Teron, and set up our family in the first registered condominium in Ontario. I tried to remind my children how lucky they were to live in a city where you can be in the wilderness in an hour but can hear and see the most beautiful works of art that you can see anywhere in the world. Now that we are such a wonderfully multi-cultural city we can savour the foods of the world and make friends with people of every race, religion, and sexual orientation without fear.

The rest is history. This is not a fairy tale. There have been divorces, tragedies and yet we all stay connected. I myself have survived cancer and am now married to the most amazing man in the world who accepts me with all of my warts and all of my extended family as I do with his. We're lucky to have each other and live in the most beautiful city in Canada.

Montreal

by Rosalie Tunis

When I think about it, and it's not often, I can't believe the age I am. In my mind, I certainly don't feel this old, even though my body tells me otherwise.

Born in 1938, I spent my childhood in the then city of Outremont, now known as part of Montreal. At that time Outremont had its own mayor and school board. I grew up in a mixed neighborhood, made up of middle and lower class Protestants, Jews and Catholics.

There were two or three churches in the area and one synagogue (which we did not attend with any frequency). The street where I spent my younger years playing, walking and making friends was an older street, one where the maple tree tops nearly met in the middle of the road. In the fall I remember jumping in the piles of colourful autumn leaves, as well as going out on Halloween in homemade costumes. We couldn't afford to buy the costumes; also, no parents accompanied us.

School for me, was an exciting place. I couldn't wait to start Kindergarten. My school was large; it took up a block and had three floors. To this day I remember each teacher I had from Grades 1 to 7 and all their names. Competition was very much encouraged and I thrived in that in that atmosphere, usually ranking first or second at nears end.

High School, Strathcona Academy, formed years of challenges, new best friends, and of course, the usual teenage anxieties. In my last three years I had a summer job at age 15, 16 and 17. My work was in a law office filling in for vacationing staff, doing filing and receptionist jobs. Also, learning to work the lines on an old-fashioned switchboard was a huge job, which was *not* fun.

Finally, I had enough money saved to attend MacDonald's teachers college—away from strict parental supervision. I was free to behave, or misbehave as I found fit- on my own for the first time in my life.

When training was over, I felt ready, at last, to tackle a teaching career. I was eighteen years old and I thought I knew everything. What I still didn't realize was that I had a lot to learn about and from life. Fortunately, due to a good upbringing I was equipped to face those challenges.

Couldn't Be Canadian

by Joan Fulthorp Jubb

My ancestors were part of the Lord Selkirk settlers that left Scotland and settled near Winnipeg.

My grandpa Fulthorp's father came from England and was one of the Father's of the Red River settlement. His mom's family came from the northern shores of Scotland, [The Highland Clearances] and so on.

When I started school and I had to learn my 'straction as my five-year-old self said it (Extraction—as you couldn't be Canadian until 1949 and since I was born in 1938, at five, it would have been 1943). When I came home from school, my mom was overwhelmed with a one-year-old and a three-year-old and my dad was away training for the Air Force. His dad was living with us and I was told to ask him. Grandpa was my hero. He loved me.

He told me that I was Canadian because I was born in Canada, my dad was born in Canada and he was born in Canada and his mother was born in Canada. I dutifully went and told all this to my teacher. She tut tutted and said, "Child you really need to learn your extraction!"

Home again and I said all this to my grandpa and he was frustrated and I now realized it was because we had a long history in Canada. He said that since his father was born in England and his mother's people were from Scotland and his wife was born in Germany of Russian and Spanish parentage, I must be Heinz 57!

Solemnly and eagerly, I trotted back to relate this wondrous information. I was Heinz 57! We never used the product and so I thought this was like all the other things he spoke of. Needless to say, the teacher was less than impressed! In fact, she thought it was demeaning that my family told me I was Heinz 57.

She did, however, discern from my tale that I was of English 'straction and I was sent back to my seat.

I was always the "tall skinny red head" who was awkward and talked too much, and was always late no matter the school's threats.

A Story of Two Amazing Men

by Paula McClure Larsen

When my granddaughter, Kelsie, mentioned this idea of writing a story about my life here in Canada I was a bit hesitant because I don't have a grand story to tell, I haven't changed the world or gone on some amazing adventure. What defines my life, and what made it worth living, were the people. Specifically two amazing men, two men who inspired me, two men who aided me in becoming the woman I am today.

The first of these two men is my father, Donald Start McClure, born on January 6th, 1923. My father was ambitious; he was driven by his love of flying. Back in that time everyone wanted to go to war, but sadly my father was too young. He didn't let that discourage him, instead he started training other men to go overseas, and because he knew he was contributing in a way, it was good enough for him. He and my mother had five children together, me being the oldest. We lived a good life. We were a middle-class family, and we didn't need much. We were happy just to have a roof over our heads and food on our plates. Unfortunately my father passed away at a rather young age, and to this day, I never stop thinking about him. I was and always will be so proud of my father, and so glad my grandchildren got to meet him before his passing.

I was in my tenth year of school, when I met the other man, the love of my life, Hans Cristian Larsen. Hans hadn't had the easy life that I had. When he was only six years-old his father left. To make ends meet, his mother ran a boarding house. Hans lived alongside 17 others; he never had a room to himself. I often think it's his struggles that made him the man he was. Being that he was in his 12th year of school, meant that I got to go to his high school graduation alongside him. That night was wonderful, the first of many memories that I will forever cherish. Hans and I got engaged at a very young age; I remember the night he went and asked my father if he could propose. My father had just gotten an important job at work that he was in a rush for, while taking out the garbage Hans saw my father and chased him down. All of my siblings were in a nearby bush dying of laughter. My father's simple response was "There better not be a wedding anytime soon."

We then moved from New Brunswick, to a small town in Newfoundland, called Gander. We didn't have much, but we had each other. When we finally did get married it was magical. Later came our two daughters, Tracy and Sherri. Then many years later they both had kids; in total we were blessed with six beautiful grandchildren. Hans and our first grandchild, Kelsie, had an extraordinary connection.

One of the most difficult experiences Hans and I had to go through, was when Tracy and four of our grandchildren moved up to Ottawa, Ontario. Hans was much more than a "family man" though, he was a "people man". He was an avid volunteer. When I think about it, I couldn't name anything he didn't volunteer for. He won dozens of awards, but there's one that really sticks out in my mind. This award was called The Melvin Jones Fellowship Award, which was awarded through The Lions Club, for his dedication to making a difference. He was so modest; he didn't think he deserved such an award. I remember him accepting it, with tears flowing down his cheeks. He was also deeply invested with helping the youth. He was president of the Boys and Girls Club for 30 years.

Myself, and these two men have dealt with our fair share of struggles. In late 2010, I was diagnosed with breast cancer. Thankfully, because of the memory of my dad, and the support of Hans, I survived. Last year, on September 6th, Hans unexpectedly passed away. I felt like his passing took away part of me. He was a very sick man for a long time, but he never let that stop him. I am so lucky to have spent my life with the most amazing man a woman could ask for. I'm so lucky to have him and my father watching over me. I am blessed with two beautiful guardian angels.

I can't say I've had a difficult life, because I haven't. Yes, there have been difficult times in my life, but they don't define me. My financial troubles don't define me; my cancer doesn't define me. I define me, and my family defines me. These two men define me. I've lived a wonderfully simple life. I didn't need to change the world, in order to have a purpose, and I know that my life will not end in oblivion.

LPOSKB – Lucky Pierre: The Original Sand Kicking Bull

by Peter Richer

I'm a French-Canadian born in 1942 and raised in Centretown in Ottawa at Laurier and Lyon. I went to *Ecole Garneau* for my first eight years and then on to Osgoode High School, which is not there any longer. I would spend my weekdays in Sandy Hill at my grandparent's house. Monday mornings I'd leave with a suitcase and some books under my arm and walk down to Laurier and over the Laurier Bridge (the trains used to come in there at one time) and turn right at Cumberland to Osgoode. Two blocks away, during the week, I would fight the Englishmen on Mann Avenue. On the weekends I'd come back to Laurier and Lyon in Centertown and spend the weekend fighting the Frenchmen. St. Jean Baptiste day I would spend at Laurier and Bronson. So I guess I was truly bilingual.

When I was 16 and I was going to St.Pat's High School, the Jackson Building blew up on Bank and Slater. There was an huge explosion; the roof blew off and crushed the houses for two blocks around. Thankfully only one person got killed. I remember our house shook. We heard later that it was a natural gas explosion and it was a grounds-keeper who flicked a switch causing the place to blow up.

After high school I drifted for a year. I got a fake ID, changed the spelling of my name and ended up working in a grain elevator outfit outside of Sioux City, Iowa. When I came back to Canada, I was a smoker and I had a dream to own a brand new 1966 MGB with roll up windows. It was the first year they built them and they cost $10,000 dollars. In order to save for the car, smoking had to go because I had five bucks to do it with. I stopped smoking for 36 months, saved the money I needed, and then went across to Carlingwood Shopping Centre to a little store that was open in those days, and bought a package of Exports and kept right on smoking. I was smoking 75 a day until I stopped again in ’91 and haven’t had a cigarette since. It doesn't bother me and other people’s smoke doesn’t bother me either, so I've got no problems.

I went on to become a magnetic surveyor at Spartan and traveled around the world in medium twin-engine planes looking for metals and was gone ten-and-half months of the year. I got married and my wife of that time travelled with me. We were married in '88 and split by ’91. Eventually I met another woman through a friend at work and we’ve been married 41 years. I did jobs for CIDA and the ministry of energy, mines and resources, met royals in Africa, and was the sole survivor, with no injuries, of two plane crashes; one in the Artic and the other in the Congo. They called me LPOSKB; Lucky Pierre the original sand kicking bull.

Eventually I came home again. I was at the Plaza Hotel reading *The Ottawa Journal* want-ads and saw a job for speedy muffler. I became the assistant manager and eventually ended up moving to Montreal as VP of Operations. That job took me traveling too. I ended up in Germany and France. Eventually the company was bought out and I was laid off. I was there 18 years. I came home, and saw another ad in the paper to work for Midas. I went to Toronto for the interview and ended up looking after all of Eastern Ontario. I was there two-and-a half years and then had an aneurysm. I tried to keep working, but it affected my memory and my sense of location so I could no longer do the job. After that I bought a house in Barrhaven and went to work for the aviation museum twice a week.

My wife Liz and I have two children. We went to Quebec City once, threw a pebble at the moon and came back pregnant and so we did it again. We all still live in Ottawa. I'm retired now and working hard on my health. I still have some flip flops from Sudan from 1968 when I was a surveyor. They are made from Michelin Tires. I paid 50 cents for them at the time.

I never missed home when I was away and I could move to anywhere in Canada and call it home. It wouldn't bother me. Even now, I'm still LPOSKB!

A Family History

by Norma Beers

It was the year 1815 when my great grandparents, William and Mary Stone Hunting journeyed from Templeton, Massachusetts with their two young daughters and a brother, Seth Hunting. They were seeking free available land for farming and a waterway for milling. With $200 between them, they finally found 500 acres. William Hunting established the original saw and grist mills and named the small town that grew up around them Huntingville. Seth chose farm land nearby and he and his family farmed there successfully for many years. They also started the Hunting Dairy which provided milk to the whole area.

They had crossed the border without incident into Canada. Borders were very unified at the time which explains why Island Park Vermont had one side of its main street in Quebec and the other side in Vermont. Likewise when my maternal grandparents gave up their farm in Hereford, Quebec, they bought a line house—one half of the house was in Canada and the other half was in the USA. The line house is now a treasured landmark.

My dad, Ken was reared by his dad as the eldest son to eventually take over the mill. High school was not considered a necessity for this, although his four younger brothers and two younger sisters went on to finish high school, with two sisters going to college and university to become teachers. My grandfather set up one son in the local store and the other three in farming. All were successful and apparently there was no sibling rivalry. Obviously at this time the rule of the eldest succeeding his father was in tact. My father completed the final grade in the one-room schoolhouse three times, not because he failed but because he wanted to keep learning. Then he was sent to the mill in Kazabazua, Ontario, to learn milling skills. He was 16-years-old and told me how lonesome he was. This hands-on approach allowed him to go into business with my grandfather and eventually to take over the business as prosper.

Customers travelled as far away as Montreal, to buy his cereals and flours. Later on he took a business course in Sherbrooke, Quebec where he met my mother.

The Hunting Family Cookbook was written in the 1930s to promote the whole wheat and corn flour produced in the mill by my father, Kenneth William Hunting. The roller mill was installed in 1909 and ceased operation in 1955 due to expansion of larger flour mills. Lillian Palmer created the recipes for the cookbook. She believed in the combination of simplicity and economy and the nutritional value in the flours and cereals that my father developed.

The lumber mill remained in the family for seven generations until my brother Ross, the final owner, sold it to a Montreal firm as he found doing business in Quebec as an Anglophone incredibly difficult, this despite the fact that he spoke French and employed many francophone. The name W. H. Hunting and Sons remained and his son Karl remained as general manager. Several years later, however, the mill was sold to an American company and Karl was let go. The mill still stands and is a very big part of milling in Canada. It was the last lumber mill in Canada still run with a water wheel.

My childhood memories of the sound of the dam, the running of the saws and the feel of the sawdust mounds on my feet are still with me to this day.

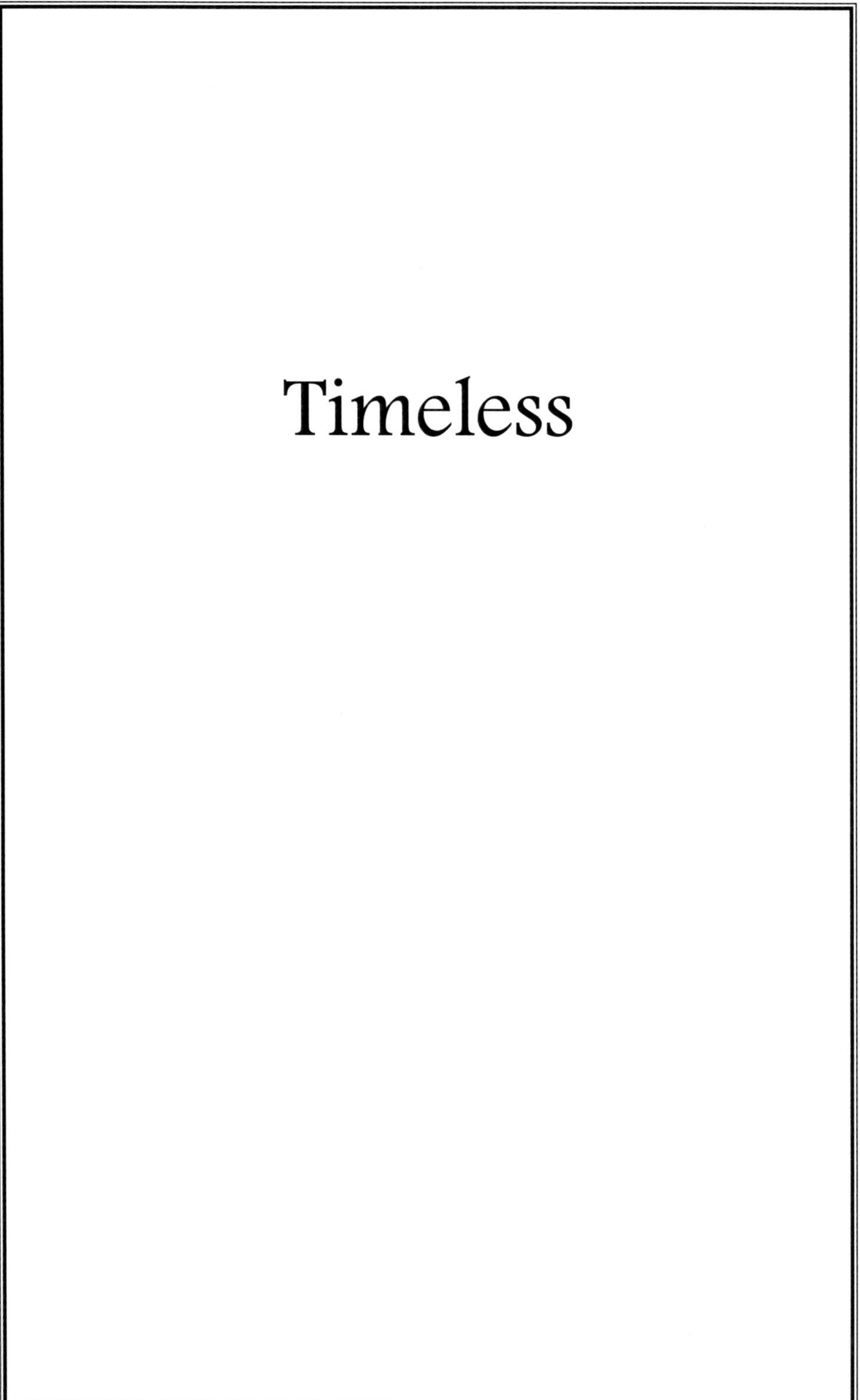

Timeless

Zombies at My Window

by Marcia Taylor

The windows of my old house in Ashton, Ontario are covered with cluster flies, dopey creatures that spend their time trying to get inside in the fall and out again in the spring. They are feckless creatures who seem to exist only to annoy.

The cluster fly is not like the mosquito which is canny and has personality. The cluster fly is stupid and sluggish and has no interesting abilities. It doesn't suck blood, or transmit deadly diseases, but instead preys upon a more modest life form, the hapless earthworm. The cluster fly lays its eggs in the soil in a newly ploughed field, so that when the curious earthworm wriggles to the surface to look around these fly offspring can attach themselves to the innocent worm and proceed to eat him up. So worms expire and I get more flies in the house. What is the point of all that?

Once inside, these flies have nothing better to do than wander around on windows and then fall to the floor, as if dead. After a few hours lying motionless they get the bright idea to fly up to the window again for another look, then back to the floor they fall again, where they may spin around on their backs for a while and then play dead for a day or two. That's the really perplexing thing about cluster flies. At any point in their life they can appear to be dead, half dead, almost dead, or nearly dead, but, like zombies, they never quite expire. How many times have I bent down to pick one off the carpet only to discover that the corpse has a few good buzzes left in him?

I once thought the cluster fly was just a run-down house fly, but real houseflies are frisky and task-oriented, determined to sit on your dinner—or whatever—any time they get the chance. Cluster flies don't give a hoot about dinner. They prefer the light bulb on the ceiling where they walk about aimlessly while considering their next moment of death. As we dine below, giant fly shadows travel around the room, giving us the impression that cars are going by. Shadows are tolerable, but we know what comes next. The butter usually breaks their fall.

Cluster flies are filled with glue. I have tried all manner of cleaning potions on the window sills to no avail, although I have removed a considerable amount of paint. Did I mention that when cluster flies really do die, they explode and leave a fine gray spray of guts in unreachable places? The only way to get rid of fly specks is to scrape them off with a fingernail, which makes for a good day of farm fun.

Those bug zapper tennis racquets are dandy for mosquitoes, although you have to be a pro to fry a genuine house fly. The cluster fly however, will land on the electric grid of its own volition. A few gleeful zaps cause it to bounce and roll about a bit, but of course it doesn't die. Instead the shock treatment seems to revive the darned thing so it can careen off to drop inside someone's collar. Funny!

The last person in the house to turn out the light is bound to be bunking with a couple of cluster flies. They love to spin around inside that halogen hell which is the reading lamp, and, being cluster flies, they don't burn to a crisp, they just bash about until near death, and then they drop out to cool off in your hair. Or, they stay very quiet until you turn out the light and then they plop onto the pillow.

The sensible thing to do is to leave the bathroom light on all night so all the flies in the house can happily congregate there, and at sun-up they can buzz on over to the window for the day. This is the time to exact my revenge, which comes in the form of glue paper. One sheet stuck to the window will catch dozens of insects in short order. They land, they stick, they buzz a bit, and then they just sit quietly . . . not quite dead of course. A small breeze will bring them all to life at once, so whenever you walk by the window a chorus of cluster flies will rise up, calling to be set free.

When the glue paper is well-populated, it's disposal time. This is not for the squeamish because as soon as those nearly dead creatures feel the motion of being carried to the bin, they all try to lift off at once, which makes the trap vibrate uncomfortably, and the hair on my arms stand on end too. I once tried to vacuum the not-quite-expired bodies off one of those pricey glue papers but all I got was a bunch of flies minus their feet. Too cruel, I decided.

One spring day, as I was removing yet another fly-laden glue paper from the bathroom window, I was surprised to see a tiny flycatcher out on the ledge, the one who has her mud nest stuck up under the eaves. She is the most successful of our yard birds, raising two batches of babies per season and returning year after year to the same nest. And she was happily pecking cluster flies off the outside screen. She eats cluster flies! Mother Nature is not crazy after all.

A Summer Hike

by Ida May Gardiner

"It's a long way to Tipperary, it's a long way to go" began our adventure. Kathy, Colleen, Kim, wee Geordie, my sister Cathy and I started hiking up the hot, dusty, gravel road on our way to the Maple Bush. We took the left-over World War II kit bag that was now stuffed full of peanut butter and jam sandwiches. Someone carried the jug of "Freshie" (probably fruit punch flavour).

When we reached the overgrown gate of our grandparent's old farm we were just finished singing "I'm a Rambler, I'm a Gambler." The homestead itself burned down years before our time and it left a basement filled with rubble, weeds and a few critters. We stopped to explore for treasure that we knew wasn't really there. We moved into the Old Barn which sagged and creaked with the warning sounds of decay, but, we were fearless and confidently walked along the beams that stretched out over the open floors. We played there often during the summers, so it wasn't long before we were ready to continue on our hike.

There was a cow-path that ran from the Old Barn through the back fields and up into the Maple Bush. Like the cows, we followed one another in single file. There was some debate over who was going to piggy-back wee Geordie, who was now exhausted and stopped on the trail. Once he had settled on my sister's back, we were soon walking and singing again. "The other day (echo), I met a bear (echo), Out in the woods (echo), A-way out there (echo)." We all knew about bears. The Warren family had a black bearskin blanket at their cottage and we had all been under it often. And so it was that we entered the Maple Bush tired, thirsty, ready to eat and thinking about bears.

We found a nice flat clearing and spread out to eat our picnic lunch. Once the sandwiches were gone and the Freshie guzzled, we lay a little dozy, looking up through the canopy. The light is tricky in the bush as it bounces between branches and leaves and casts shadows that are not familiar to young visitors. Sound has a funny way of travelling through the trees and can be more than a little deceiving. A chipmunk can make a huge racket as it digs for food and a deer can wander about silently. It's hard to say who saw it first, or heard it first but we were all shortly up the nearest tree with shouts of "BEAR!"

Clinging to the branches for our very lives, we looked this way and that. Shadows moved and we were certain we were going to die. After what seemed like eternity, we grew tired waiting for the bear to charge us and soon began to talk about making a run for it. Our biggest problem was wee Geordie. Could he make it? And, how much trouble would we be in if the bear ate him?

Alternate Camping Facilities for Senior Physicians

by Dick Lewis

As a semi-retired physician who has served an average of 5,000 patients per year for over four decades, getting away for a camping holiday each summer is mandatory for maintenance of health and sanity. As a father of eight, regular time off is a necessity.

There are some of us who prefer an "all inclusive", but with the many conveniences of a Winnebago camper, others may prefer all the amenities in a park-like setting with the camaraderie of fellow campers.

But my favourite getaway is as a solo camper, on an isolated lake an hour by float plane north of Whitehorse, Yukon, at the end of August when the bugs are all hibernating.

With a simple A-frame cabin, with wood stove, propane appliances, boat and motor, and satellite phone for emergencies, there is no need for any other electronics. And no one else is on the lake.

When I have unloaded my food, booze, fishing gear, camera, carving tools, etc., and checked my satellite phone battery, I wave goodbye to my pilot Bernard, and begin my week off with a ritual I've performed each arrival day for the last ten summers—I remove my watch, store it in one of the kitchen drawers, and start unwinding.

The water from the lake must be boiled before consumption, and the two-seater outhouse is about a hundred yards away. At night however, we older folks need to go more often. And I'm quite content to use a container which comes in handy the next morning. That is when I mark my territory by pouring the contents on all large trees starting about six feet up the tree. The reason for this is to signal to any large nocturnal animals that another creature, much taller than any bear or wolf, has control of the cabin area and that is one of two deterrents I use.

Another benefit on lone camping is that I can eat all the beans I want, something I avoid back home.

Weather permitting my daily fishing regimen is mostly successful with a choice of seven species to challenge with my selection of handmade flies. I am also careful to clean fish on the other side of the lake so as to avoid attracting grizzlies. But I don't bother with bear whistles, bangers, sprays, or other traditional techniques that the Wildlife Conservation Officers recommend.

No, I just make sure that I practice my clarinet twice a day.

Canoeing

by Gerard Lewis

My wife, Louise, and I set out for Kingston. Our low-gunwale fibreglass canoe was laden with tent, sleeping bags, cooking implements, and food. We headed upstream to the Rideau Lakes intent on travelling on through the downstream of the Cataraqui. Our seven-day trip ran along a 202 mile waterway connecting two capitals. Twelve miles of canal, 45 locks at 23 lock stations, lifted us up166 feet and let us down 275. We camped at lock stations, a provincial park, and a friend's cottage at far side of the headwaters called the Rideau Lakes. On day three we awoke at Murphy's Point on a calm cloudless summer day, the Big Rideau - a mirror to God's daytime universe. Declaring it to be our day of rest, we absorbed every soothing ray of warm sunshine. At nightfall we gazed at a galaxy of stars above our heads and the sparklers of a crackling fire at our feet. Reward preceeded a day of high risk and arduous exertion.

The next day we woke to white caps and a stiff wind in our face. On a calm day our low-gunwale canoe was inches above the waterline. On this day, inches lapsed into centimetres. Waves lapped into peril. Undaunted or plain stupid, we pressed on to our destination: Lake Opinicon, a log cabin, friends and hot water.

The trip lasted 12 hours and covered 22 miles not in a straight line. We could only paddle safely with the winds directly in front of us; and the winds shifted all day long. The worst stretch involved tacking into the wind then with the wind at our back then back and forth. Zig-zagging our way added miles, muscle and fortitude. Looking straight ahead was not easy. Looking back was out of the question. We pressed on, and as we did, my mind harkened to an earlier time in my life.

My first experience paddling a canoe was when I was 10 or 11. I spent two weeks at Camp Ondadawak a YMCA camp on the shores of Golden Lake in Ontario. My father had suffered the first of a series of heart attacks when I was 10. He and my mother needed recovery time. God felt that I needed to learn survival skills. I needed to be a boy freely growing up in nature—although it would be years later before I understood the latter.

A newspaper review of the camp program describes the two most notable program highlights: the overnight canoe trip. Bantams like me would set out on a two-day overnight across the wide expanse of Golden Lake to Connors Rock or as some titteringly referred to it—Ronner's Cock. Three cabins, three junior and three senior counsellors, and 24 bantams set out in a tiny armada of four regular and two oversized transporter canoes; the latter we referred to as "war canoes". The winds whipped across the lake from over our left shoulders blowing us north and up the eastern shore and away from our destination. The lighter two-and three-man canoes would eventually find themselves in a position to double back into the wind and over to the campsite, a longer stretch but doable.

The high gunwales of the war canoes however made following the smaller canoes impossible. To plow across to the western shore with the wind trapped against the high gunwales, nose and tail of this battleship of a canoe would challenge the most fit of the most experienced voyageurs. We were ten, eleven-year-old paddlers, one junior and one senior counsellor. We would have to find other means. We would sail. We would sail as Vikings. It was the most spectacular, adventuresome, exhilarating way to get across on that day.

First we beached our vessel at a stretch of eastern shoreline on Crown land. The acreage was low and filled with thin trunk trees: young poplar and other varieties. Two were felled; one taller than the other; one with a wider base than the other—about 5 inches in diameter. One would serve as a mast; the other as the crossbeam from which a red blanket—aka a square sail—could be draped.

If you know anything about war canoes you will know that the bow thwart—a piece of wood between the gunwales near the front of the vessel, is designed with a six inch hole through which a makeshift mast can be inserted and set upon the keel where a block with a shallow six inch diameter cup holds the mast in place preventing it shifting.

Rigged and ready to trap a side wind, the bottom left and right tips of our sail tied to two lanyards held in place by the junior counsellor, the senior counsellor manning his broad tailed canoe paddle at the ready to his left, we pushed off for the opposite shore. Immediately the angled-sail picked up a full pocket of steady wind. The lanyards taught, we steadily moved forward, bantam Vikings holding paddles on our laps, sitting sunk down and pressed against the hull, the transporter rising above the whitecaps. Screaming and howling we rode a rough ride full of bumps and thumps for a full twenty minutes. With arms weakening and the western shore with its tall and magnificent pines within our grasp, we reached the lee of the western shore and calm waters. Dead reckoning we were less than a half kilometre from Connors Rock.

So we made it, set up camp, fanned fires and grilled hot dogs and frozen burgers with all the fresh fixings provided for our first night on our own, sleeping in our tents below the stars, free men of the woods—On-da-da-waks. Until, for me and other bigger 11-year-olds, the next morning.

A sleepy camper among our cadre woke early still embracing his foggy brain, pressed himself to semi-wakefulness, urged on by a full bladder into the foggy air of our campsite, tripped and fell front teeth first onto the unforgiving granite landscape known as the Canadian shield.

A platoon of us bigger kids was mustered to take our injured comrade by war canoe back to the infirmary at Camp On-da-da-waks. Thankfully the winds of the day before had abated. We left by 9:30 and arrived by noon, in time for lunch. Or so we thought.

We were not expected since we were on our overnight. There was no place for us at the dinner table. We were given oranges, chips, and not much more that I can recall. We headed back to Connors Rock.

When we arrived for the second time to Connors Rock, we were ravenous. Day two of the overnight camping trip is devoid of fresh produce or meats. Day two is about roughing it and appreciating the marvels of cooking packages of dehydrated food. Only, there was something not working itself out over the fire pit. For reasons unknown to any of us, including the counsellors, three hours of boiling water was insufficient to turn hard flakes of whatever, into soft edible dinner for 30. And that was all we had been given and all of it has been dumped into the pot and none of it cooked. Then, under the boastful pronouncements along the lines of "I'm so hungry I will eat anything" a few bantam Vikings retched, some because of the food, others because they retch at the sight of someone else retching.

The counsellors threw in the towel, some literally to help clean up the weaker stomachs in the group, all of them metaphorically. The camp was struck. The flotilla headed for home. At 7:00 pm under an increasingly darkening sky. With all flashlights carefully packed deep in waterproof river bags.

In pitch darkness in the middle of a moonless night on the wide expanse of Golden Lake two miracles took place. The first miracle was preceeded by the sound of a large outboard motor breaking the pristine silence of our paddlers with ever louder noise indicating with every bounce that someone was headed directly at us and likely through us like a bowling ball headed down the alley. Fortunately the driver skirted by us but not without noticing our silhouettes off his starboard. He stopped and after a few frantic expletive deleted words to our counsellors agreed to circle us with his lights on. That was miracle number one.

Miracle number two. We were in the middle of the lake in complete darkness without a clue as to where we were headed because it was that dark and it was impossible to figure out the difference between a cottage here and there and a camp cabin here or there. And for some reason, the outdoor florescent lights that normally throbbed with humming and blue light at the camp dockside were extinguished. Then, just as we felt we were doomed, the reason why the camp was in total darkness became apparent: Bonfire Night. On the beach, bonfires began to burst forth to life. First one, then another, and another, in all more than a dozen bonfires strung out along the beach next to the docks we were searching for.

When we arrived, our crew of paddlers, the ones along with me who had over the course of 36 hours, paddled, sailed, then paddled twice more across a 20 mile lake, made our way into the dock area. Our adventure came to an end. We were excused from having to schlep our gear to our cabin. I remember being somewhat delirious when I arrived and parked my weary carcass on a picnic table next to our cabin and near the paddleboard tennis courts.

Most of that evening and much of the rest of my two weeks at Camp On-Da-Da-Waks is contained in a blurry bag of fond memories. My canoe trip however remains vivid in all its details. I think of it every time I enter a canoe.

It was around 6:30 when the winds finally subsided at the Rideau Lakes. At 7:00 that morning from Murphy's Point on the Big Rideau Louise and I headed to the Upper Rideau Lake, through the Newboro lock to Newboro Lake, then Clear Lake, Indian Lake and Chaffey's Lock, to the Cameron's cottage on Lake Opinicon.

Two canoe trips.

Unforgettable.

The epitome of a Canadian odyssey begins in a canoe.

Hockey

by Michele Gauthier

He was the 13th child of a family of 15 children in St. Irenée, in the rural area of Charlevoix, Quebec, born in 1914. As a child, he would go with his brothers up to the mountain lake, a few kilometers away to skate. They would make the trek in snowshoes, carrying skates and shovel. They had to remove the snow from the lake before they could engage in their favorite past-time. The goals consisted of two rocks. There was no warm shed to change in, no Tim's coffee to warm them up. Nevertheless they revelled in playing Canada's favorite sport.

His hockey prowess earned him a scholarship at the seminary in Bathurst, New Brunswick.

After the war, Félix moved to Schefferville in northern Quebec to work for the airport. Schefferville is a remote town, 365 miles due north of Sept-Isles. There is no road access, only once a week air service with Quebecair or the Iron Ore Company private railway.

Of course, Félix is an avid fan of the Montreal Canadians, the Habs. He would not miss a match for the world. It is as much a sacred time in the household as was Sunday morning church.

In the 1950s, there was no cable television, no satellite. The only way to catch the Saturday night game was on the radio. Félix would sit in his lazy-boy in the living room, alone, sending his wife and daughter to play cards in the kitchen. No distraction, no talking in the living room. He didn't even want to get together with the other fellows, because they would talk too much, he had to concentrate. If one peeked to see him, one would think he was actually on the ice. Feet planted on the ground, most of the time, he would move with the players, skirt, and shoot the imaginary puck. He seemed more exhausted at the end of the game than Jean Béliveau and his teammates.

Then in the late 1960s innovation came to Schefferville, one could actually watch the Habs game on TV. The programming would come down once a week by plane. All of the programs were on a reel, like at the movie theater but fed through the local TV station. There was one problem, the Habs game would not be the current Saturday night game, but the game of the week before, and it was aired, of course, at 8:00 p.m. on Saturday night. So, he would have to choose between listening to the current game on the radio, or watching the game of the previous week on the television. This did not phase Félix at all, he could multi-task. So, the living room became on Saturday night like a church, no talking, no whispering, just listening intently with his eyes riveted on the TV His pace seemed to pick up too. He would move, shoot, skirt another imaginary player constantly. It seemed to me that he was "off synch" sometimes because his movements, his reaction didn't match what was going on on the TV. That was because he was reacting to the radio commentary, then he would seamlessly pick up the action on the TV and continue his mime. He no longer seemed more exhausted than Jean Béliveau, he truly was as he was playing two games at once.

At 99, Félix is still avid about hockey, never misses a match on TV or one of his grand-sons' games.

Reaping

by Caroline O'Leary Hartwick

There are Christmas memories that at times you would like to forget and then you realize how important they are. Christmas at my home growing up was all about sharing and giving. Most of our gifts were homemade, and everyone was expected to help in the preparations. My mother and father, who were actually my grandparents, assigned tasks to everyone. I, however, didn't like helping out with any kind of preparations; I just didn't feel I should have to.

My tasks were left undone as I sat daydreaming about all the delicious treats that would be in my stocking on Christmas. Oranges, large red apples, specially wrapped candies and other delicacies, which were rare in our house partly because there wasn't much money, and special things were not available in the winter. Being in my dream world I did not hear my Grandfather approach and with a frown. He looked down at the task at hand. "Not getting much done here, Caroline?" I just continued to sit there lazily shifting things around. Grandfather grumbled a warning, "Ya know little one, Santa don't bring all those fancy treats yous are dreaming about to children that don't listen and do as they're told; ya could just get a big stick instead."

Being a tenacious child I seldom wanted to listen and often went my merry way, daydreaming about all those special treats with my grandfather giving a warning grumble now and then. Everyone was busy preparing for the Christmas season (except me) with decorating, baking and making of gifts. The house always smelled delicious. Grandmother also had the job of decorating the church and I was supposed to help, but I doubt that I did.

A few days before Christmas grandfather trudged into the back woods and cut down a beautiful spruce tree to decorate. Grandmother liked spruce trees best as they were easier to decorate. I was expected to help, but I doubt that I did. On Christmas Eve I was really excited as I hung my stocking up behind the wood stove. Back then we just used plain woolen stockings and not the fancy ones that are used today. Again, Grandfather grumbled, but I payed little, if any heed. What, in fact, did he know, I thought condescendingly? Christmas was very magical with all the lights and now that we had electricity it was even more magical. I found it difficult to get settled down for the night and was very tiresome, Grandfather grumbled.

Christmas morning finally arrived all sparkling and white and very cold. I could hear Grandfather moving around downstairs lighting the fires, going out to feed the animals and bringing in wood for the stoves. There was never a day off at the farm. I was excepted to help, but I doubt that I did.

When the house was finally warm and I could smell Grandmother's delicious cooking I tip toed down the stairs. In order to get to the kitchen I had to pass the beautiful lit Christmas tree and the wood stove where all stockings were hanging. They were bulging with beautiful treats and candy canes hanging out with knitted mittens on the side, so full of all the joys. Only one stood rather flat with no candy cane, no mittens just a rather large splintery wooden stick blaring at me out of the top of my old wool sock. I stood transfixed, that one was mine, I knew! I was horrified and burst into tears. "No, Nooo, not fair!" I blubbered. Grandfather grumbled," You may be able to fool yaself, but ya can't fool Santa." A lesson I've had to relearn many times in my life. You reap what you sow!

Adoption

by Marilyn O'Neill

My father was notorious for bringing strangers home. One Saturday I remember he had been downtown Montreal and picked up two sailors to whom he gave a tour of the city and then brought them to our home for a meal and then took them back to their ship. He always encouraged me to bring my friends home and to host parties and at these parties I would often find my friends upstairs talking and joking with my parents.

Living in this welcoming environment I always hounded my parents to adopt a child or at least bring an orphan home for the holidays. (I did have a brother, seven years younger than I, but he didn't seem to fit the bill). Rightfully so, my parents would always explain that it would not be fair to a child to bring them home for a celebration and then take them back to the orphanage.

I was married in Sept. 1970 and we moved to Vancouver. My husband and I had an agreement that once we had $5,000 in the bank we would think about starting a family. In July 1973 we found out we were going to have a baby and we were elated (we had $5,000 in the bank for about a day). Our beautiful daughter was born in April 1974.

We tried to have a second child but to no avail. It was a couple of years later when I started mentioning to my husband that perhaps we should adopt a child. His answer was always if God granted us one beautiful healthy little girl that is all we are meant to have. Another year passed and I continued to be discouraged every month. One night we were getting ready to attend a party and Naomi Bronstein was on

TV talking about all the children she had brought over from Korea for different operations plus there was an interview with a priest who ran an orphanage in South Korea. Both my husband and I watched the show and then went off to the party where, as fate would have it, one of the families that had hosted a child from Korea was in attendance. We chatted for awhile and, by the time we returned home, my head was reeling. The next morning I started talking to my husband about all we had learned about Korea and adoption. I couldn't believe it, at this point my husband said OK why don't you look into it. I think I flew to the phone and started the process.

It took two years from start to finish to receive our beautiful five-year-old daughter. My father and I travelled to New York City to pick up our daughter while my husband and daughter waited anxiously for our return.

Our daughter arrived in New York very tired but with the cutest little smile on her face. At first I thought what if I can't love this little girl? It only took minutes before I realized that she had stolen my heart and I felt that I was the luckiest woman on the planet. Many people have said to us what a lucky little girl our adopted daughter was, to which I respond what a lucky family we are, for she completed our family. A quote I read years ago pertaining to adopted children was "my child was not born from beneath my heart but from my heart".

Captured Moments

Ottawa River Recollections

by Earl Lytle

These recollections take place on the Ottawa River in Ottawa West just east of Woodroffe Avenue, about 1945 to 1950. Both Bert and I were between 7 and 12 years of age at this time. We lived on Richmond Road in a series of houses bordered by the road and streetcar tracks in front and behind by the railroad tracks. Several doors west of us was "Leaflour Brothers Coal, Coke and Ice" which was a fuel and ice business. On the other side of the streetcar tracks was a cow pasture and wooded area. This was part of the Honeywell farm. The actual farm buildings were at the site of the present day Carlingwood Shopping Centre.

Cleary Street ran to the river at this time near the present site of the Unitarian Church. We were playing along the shore in early spring when the ice was melting. I got trapped on an ice floe that started to drift away from the shore. Bert with a mighty leap joined me on the floe. He did it, I'm sure out of friendship and not wanting to miss an adventure. It was a very scary time and we huddled together and yelled for help. However, no help arrived. We were very lucky as the floe gradually drifted back to shore about 100 yards to the east. We jumped ashore at the lodge and ran home to tell the exciting tale to our friends.

On another occasion we went swimming at Deschenes beach on a beautiful summer day. The beach was located a few hundred yards west of Cleary St. For some reason we decided to swim out to the boom logs about 100 yards out in the river. The boom was a series of logs chained together to contain and direct logs floating down the river to the Eddy mill. We had just learned to swim and were certainly not good swimmers at the time.

We reached the boom and after resting a while decided to swim back to shore. We were very tired and wondered if we would make it. We struggled on and went through a large weed bed. The weeds seemed to grab us. We were exhausted but fought to reach the shore. Bert was behind me and suddenly I heard him start to laugh. I looked back and he was standing up in knee deep water. We happily walked to shore and lay on the beach laughing.

The next vignette took place on the river about 100 yards out from the end of Cleary Street. In the winter, Leaflour Bros. cut ice from the river and stored the blocks under sawdust. They sold the blocks to families who used iceboxes. The ice was brought by horse sled to their large storage sheds.

Bert and I ventured out one Sunday to their ice cutting shack on the river. We were invited in by one of the workers who had his girlfriend there. The cutting operation was closed on Sunday and they were there enjoying a few drinks. It was a sunny day but quite cold in the shack.

She ventured outside wearing a large fur coat. We heard a scream followed by lots of swearing. We went outside to find she had fallen through the ice in one of the recently cut stripes. Only her head and shoulders were above water. Luckily she had put her arms out as she fell or she could have went right under. Her boyfriend gradually pulled her out but she was mad as hell as well as being soaking wet. They got in their car parked by the shack and slowly drove away. We heard her berating him for a considerable distance. It was not a perfect date.

One summer day we decided to go fishing and borrowed a boat that was kept at the end of Cleary Street. We rowed the boat west then out to the booms. We found a boom log with a partially submerged end. With one of us in the back we ran the bow onto the boom. At this point we both got out on opposite sides and pulled the boat to the other side of the boom log.

In the middle of the river was a large deadhead. This was a log with one end stuck on the bottom and the other end above water. It was a huge log as the river was 40 to 50 feet deep and the visible end was 10 feet above the water line.

On reaching the deadhead we tied the boat to it and commenced fishing. We used hand lines with a large sinker and two baited hooks. The bait of choice were dew worms which we picked at night from the front lawn.

We usually caught about a dozen or more channel catfish about a pound or two each. Sometimes we brought up five-foot long green eels. They were a bit scary and difficult to unhook because they were very slimy and hard to hold onto. They also constantly twisted their bodies. We were glad to get them back into the river.

Our return trip consisted of using the same technique of crossing the boom and rowing to shore. Here we cleaned the fish and proudly carried them home. Another fine day had been provided by the Ottawa River.

Election Day

by Linda Wilson

Election Day on the Florida Road, and, no doubt in countless other communities in rural Nova Scotia during the 1940's and 50's, brought with it both tension and excitement. People who would today be considered far less than sophisticated took great interest in the political activities and climate of the time. Livelihoods were dependent on which party controlled the paving of roads or clearing of snow, and government contracts for these and other projects were much sought after. People held strong views, which they were quick to defend at the slightest provocation. Everyone up and down the road knew who his neighbours would be voting for—it was a matter of history and habit. The Kirk's always voted Liberal, and made no bones about it.

The big draw was the process. Chores were done early on Election Day, and supper was a hurried affair. Then the waiting began in earnest, until somebody spied a strange car turning into the lane. "They're here!" someone would shout. The men grabbed their coats and gathered out in the big entry room, as the driver made his way in. The sight of his bulging pocket, with maybe a bit of brown paper just visible, brought hearty greetings from the men. The women tightened their apron strings—and their smiles. There was no point in arguing. This was how it was done. The bottle made its way around the circle of waiting hands, while crisp two dollar bills were slipped into pockets, to appease the women's disapproval. With much backslapping and laughter they all piled into the waiting car and set off to do their electoral duty.

Memories of Life in Shawinigan Falls Quebec in the 1940s

by Mary Etta Devlin

White shoe polish has a distinct odour, at least it does to me. That smell transports me back to warm summer days when white baby boots and toddler sandals sat drying in the sun, while their owners had their afternoon naps. Even then, when I was cleaning those little shoes the smell put me in a reminiscing frame of mind. Tuesday night was band night; the smell of white shoe polish wafted from our kitchen where my mother was applying it to my Mary Janes.

Band night was a big deal! Everyone dressed in their Sunday best. The men wore collars and ties, the women wore hats that complimented their floral dresses and of course white shoes and gloves. Even the babies in their carriages were dressed in their finest. Frilly-lace trimmed dresses and bonnets for the girls and silk rompers with matching caps for the boys.

The bandstand in the centre of the park, was sparkling white. A perfect backdrop for the musicians in their bright red jackets with gold epaulettes and gold braid trim. White belts and trousers and, if my memory serves me right, military style caps with red and gold trim. Just writing about it brings back that wonderful feeling of excitement I always experienced when they started to tune up their instruments. The bandstand itself was a two-storey structure. The musicians sat above, while on the ground floor the refreshment booth sold hot dogs, French fries and ice cream, the real stuff.

We usually think of a warm summer evening with the scent of grass and flowers in the air. That was not the case on Tuesday summer evenings in Shawinigan Falls. The wonderful smell of french fries floated on the air all around the park and even on streets close by, announcing to one and all, that it was band night.

While my shoes were drying my mom braided my hair. Since this was an important event, the braids were folded up and tied with bows close to my head. Of course, the bows had been ironed that afternoon along with the outfit I was to wear and naturally, they were colour coordinated.

How sorry I am for those of you who are too young to have experienced band night in the late 1930s and 1940s.

When I was all ready, my friend Joanne was at the door. She had her nickel and my mom gave me a nickel and off we went.

I lived on First Street across from the park. My grandparents lived on Second Street across from the park. That is where we headed as we knew Nin Nin and Alex (that is what I called my grandparents, but that is another story) would be expecting us. After telling us that we looked lovely, they gave us each ten cents as usual. The dimes bought us paper bags of greasy, salty, french fries. When we finished those, the nickels were spent on ice cream, and the band played on.

We strolled around licking our cones and trying to make them last without melting all over our fine clothes. We met our friends and waved to our parents. How innocent life was then! I went to band concerts from the time I was a baby until I was nine years-old when we moved to Montreal. I was very disappointed that the park near our new home did not have a band stand or band night and none of my new friends had ever heard of band night.

Life does come full circle or close to it. Friday afternoon is band afternoon here at the Senior's Centre which I love to attend every week. I also enjoy the jazz band at the Royal Oak every other Sunday

I don't have enough hair to braid and it does cost more than fifteen cents for refreshment, but I still love the music and the time spent with friends. I don't have Mary Janes to clean but I do have running shoes and I use white polish on them. That smell still brings happy memories to mind.

War Time Baby

by Janet Beers

Although I don't personally remember WW2, being born in 1944, I grew up with such vivid stories from both of my parents that I often felt that I had been born 20 years too late. To this day my favorite music is all from the Big Band Era and the time of the jazz greats. I could sing the lyrics from most of the Rogers and Hammerstein, Lerner and Loew musicals as well as a good portion of Gilbert and Sullivan. I clearly remember when *Hockey Night in Canada* was a family affair shared by everyone from grandparents and parents to dating teenagers.

Still in my very early years in Huntingville, Quebec there were other very clear pictures. My Uncle Ross was actually only 20 years old and still single and living with his parents, when we moved from my grandparent's house after the war, to the house across the river, behind the planing mill. I would go to my grandmother's house and drive him crazy when he was trying to rest up for or from a date. During this period he taught me my first swear words to annoy my mother "Goddamn, shit, poop." I got very proficient at this series and embarrassed my mother no end. I also remember my father running from the top floor of our house across the river from my grandparent's house to the basement to put coal in the furnace and yelling all the way. He always was of the belief that if he were awake then the whole world should suffer too.

As I look back there were some life forming milestones for me. Although I was only two years old, I know that this is a memory and not something I have been told. I woke up in my crib and standing up I saw flames across the river from our house and I knew, with complete certainty, that my grandparents' house was burning. I cried and cried and nobody came. I later was told that it was the Blacksmith's Shop and that my parents had rushed across the river to be sure that it wasn't spreading to my grandparent's house

There are also many memories surrounding my grandparents' piano. Somehow this was a fascination for me right from the start! I used it as a tool to torture my uncle Ross as a baby and then I remember this wonderful friend of my parents' who sat and played and held me on his knee and made me fell so beautiful even at that age. As I grew older and we moved to Ottawa and I actually took lessons my grandparents would insist on hearing every piece I knew each time I went to visit. My mother had been a singer and dancer in her youth and I learned one of the songs that she sang at weddings called *Oh Promise Me.* Another song which, for some reason caught my fancy, was *Were You There When They Crucified My Lord* which greatly amused everyone but my Uncle Ross, whom I was still happy to annoy should he lie down for a rest on any occasion.

As I grew older and eventually started a family of my own and took them to visit, the piano was still a place of peace and fun. They sang nursery rhymes, then rock songs, then rap for their fading great grandparents beside that wonderful piano which, although never quite in tune, still maintained a richness of sound that I have rarely heard since. When my grandparents finally died the piano went to my brother, Art, as I already had my own and didn't have the room for another. The important thing was that it stayed in the family.

Chocolate

by Michèle Gauthier

My father, Félix Gauthier, was born in 1914, he will celebrate his 100th birthday this August. He has not eaten chocolate for 95 years.

He was born the 13th child of a family of 15 children in St. Irenée, in the rural area of Charlevoix, Quebec. His parents were farmers, so everyone had to contribute to the household. The boys were assigned farming chores. The girls helped in the kitchen, the garden, and with the sewing, the knitting, the laundry, the cleaning and of course, the raising of the younger siblings.

Each child had two sets of clothes, the daily clothes and the Sunday church clothes. New clothes were extremely rare, the younger kids only got hand-me-downs from the older siblings. The same went for the one pair of shoes which were mended and remended until it was no longer possible to "save" them.

Félix's eldest sister, Marie, was also his godmother. This was special. Marie was married to Arthur Gauthier. Yes, a Gauthier married another Gauthier, but they were not related. When Marie started her family, Félix was sent to her house to help her and her husband with the kids and the chores. It was not that far away, on the same concession road, or *Rang*, just down the road by buggy ride or a nice hour walk.

He loved it at Marie's house; it was quiet, just Marie and her husband with a wee one and not the hustling and bustling household of his parents. He truly cherished all of his time at Marie's house. He would often stay overnight, in his own room, in his own bed! No sharing of anything at Marie's house!

Birthdays were not really something special in terms of celebration. There were no lavish gifts. It could be a hand-made toy made by dad or the older brothers, or a knitted pair of socks or a piece of clothing made for Mom or an older sister. Money was very tight, and it was the First World War so goods of any kind were very scarce.

To celebrate Félix's fifth birthday, Marie sent away an order to the Paquet Store in Quebec City for a very special gift. The Paquet store was, at the time, the equivalent of Holt Renfew. This was quite a lavish gift for a child so young but she didn't care, he was her godchild, she adored him and he adored her.

Finally, the present arrived. Marie could not contain herself to give Félix his gift. On his birthday, she took him aside to give him his gift in private at his parent's house. It was such a special moment. Félix opened the box with anticipation. What could be hidden in the beautiful Paquet store package? A piece of new clothing, a shiny metal toy? His bright blue eyes grew bigger and bigger when he saw his present. He could not believe his eyes. A present just for him and so luxurious! When he leapt and hugged Marie, she had tears in her eyes, and so did he. He knew that she must have scraped and saved and gone without for herself and her husband to be able to afford this gift.

It was a pound of dark chocolate!

Now, there was a problem, a big problem. He only had one pound of chocolate. There were 14 siblings and two parents to share with. Not to mention brothers-in-law, sisters-in-law, cousins, aunts and uncles. What should he do? If he shared with all of them, there would be hardly any left for him. He couldn't hide it and take a small piece at a time, because if anyone else found out, they would raid his hidden sweets. There was only one solution. He hid in the closet and ate the whole thing in one sitting!

The Christmas Trunk

by Margaret Amyotte

As I age, somehow along the way I seem to have lost the magic of Christmas, that childlike excitement that I used to feel as a child growing up in Kirkland Lake, ON. Maybe it's because Christmas has been so commercialized, that I tend to reminisce about the old days in order to capture the spirit of this great feast day.

One of the brightest recollections of my childhood was of a Christmas trunk. Our maternal Grandmother used to send us a box of ribbon candies for as long as I can remember, and it always came a week or so before Christmas. We waited in anticipation as Christmas Eve arrived and no traditional box was in sight. Each time the phone rang, one or two of us would rush to answer it, and ended up being disappointed.

We were about to give up, when at 10:30 that morning, the phone rang. This time it was the train station, stating that there was a trunk from Massachusetts for us. They asked if we could come by and pick it up as soon as possible. Well, needless to say, Dad got the neighbor who owned a pick-up truck to drive him to the station. They were back home, inside of an hour. It was a big brown trunk with a whole lot of stickers on it. By the time Mom and Dad had them taken off, it was lunch time. So, of course, we had to eat. Then, we had to help mom with the household chores, which we did at an unusually fast pace.

Now finally the time had come to open the trunk. Seven of us, ranging in age from years one to 12, gathered around waiting eagerly. The trunk was opened. Inside there were a few winter clothing items, boxes of wrapped gifts, and of course, the famous box of ribbon candy, among other kinds of goodies. Our excitement was quickly turned into disappointment as Mom announced that it was time for an early supper, if we were to go to midnight mass, and thank God for our fortune. Mom closed the trunk, and said that we could wait until Christmas Day, and it would be an even bigger surprise with the gifts that Santa had for us. To ease our frustration, Mom allowed us to open one gift, which was brand new winter boots and socks that the two older children proudly wore to church.

As much as we tried to concentrate during mass, our thoughts stayed glued to what surprises waited for us under the tree. Mind you, the church choir sang its best. The nativity scene brought me back to reality, as little baby Jesus laid there looking so real, and I then realized that it was his birthday, and not mine.

After a couple of hours we were back home to a scrumptious reveillon meal that Mom had prepared for us. At each place was a glass of wine, ours being much smaller than that of our parents, of course, to toast to the occasion—the only time we were allowed such frivolity. It was already past three o'clock in the morning when we retired to bed, only to be awakened by our younger brothers' and sisters' commotion at 6:00 am, ripping the paper of whatever they thought was theirs.

Mom and Dad, quickly interrupting, giving them each their gift. I stared in awe at my gift. A beautiful red dress, accompanied with new shoes and a necklace. To top it all off, under the tree was a little red riding hood doll from Santa. Mom had made the outfit, because it was my favorite fairytale. So, who cared if I was 12 years-old? Better late than never, right! On the tree hung our Christmas stockings filled with goodies. All this, and the winter clothes we received from our relatives in the States.

This Christmas had come at a time when Dad had been off work for three weeks because of an emergency operation. There were innumerable such occasions, but this one is the most memorable. It reminds me that no matter how grim things seem to be, there is always someone who cares.

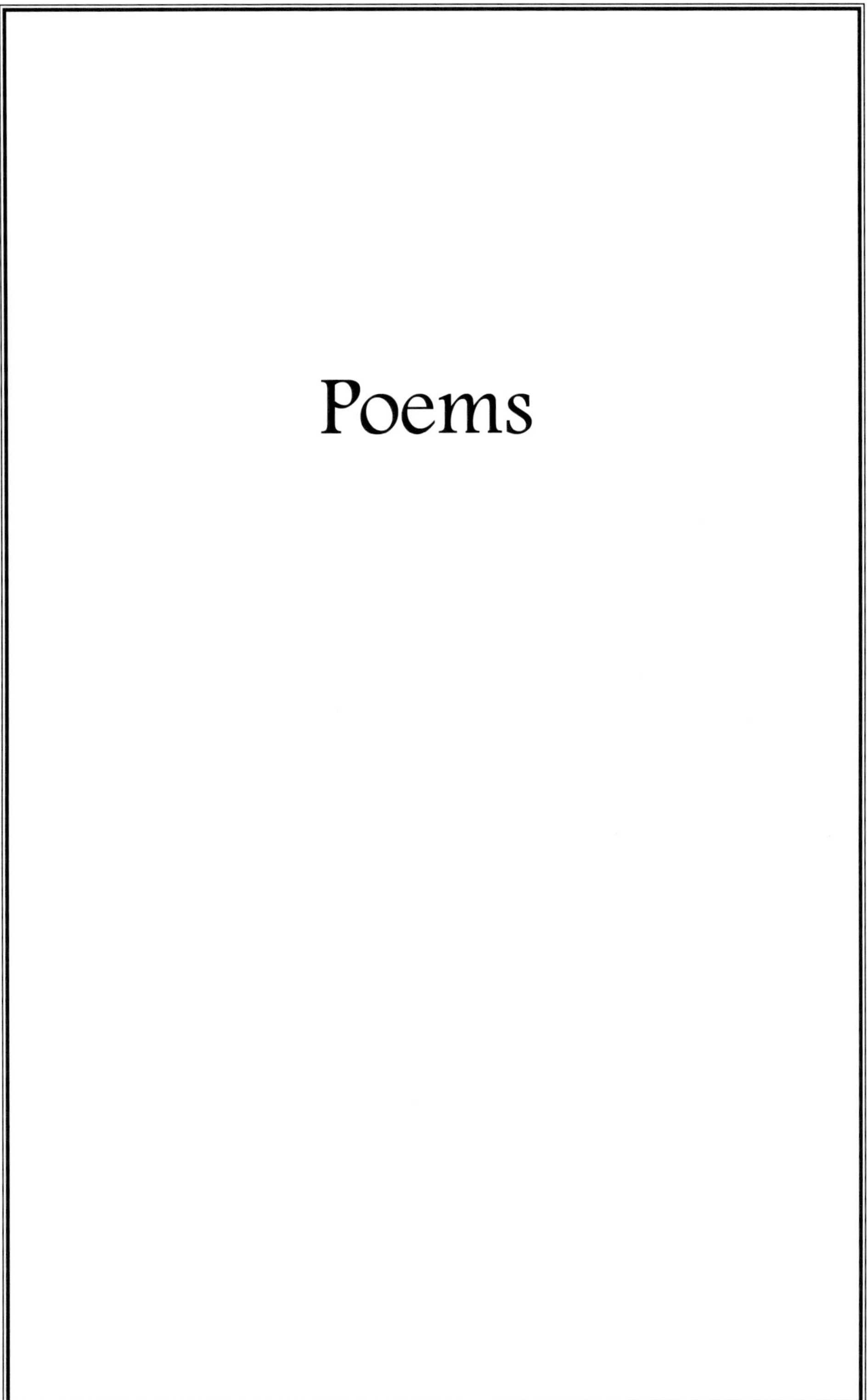

Poems

The Beaver

by Janet Beers

Industrious, ingenious, creative,
Symbol of our country,
Is it possible that even you Have adolescent angst?
Trees are falling, scattered,
Unused for your lodges.
Half chewed trunks Oozing life giving sap
Lie forlornly, left to rot
As you move, bored
To the next new challenge.
Severed giants fall aimlessly
Onto hydro wires and helpless docks.
Perhaps a young beavers' drop in center,
Pool hall, sweat lodge,
Rehabilitation center for acid rain
Could stop this ecological waste
And keep angry, armed cottagers
Temporarily at bay.

Encounter

by Bobby Salvin

"What are you going to do today?" asked my daughter
while fixing her hair.
"Today with my camera I'm going to hunt for a shot of a
live Yukon bear."
And so I set out for Decades Lake, a place where the
berries are lush.
With the gas tank full, my camera in hand and an eager eye
on the bush.
I drove along happily, senses alert, my thoughts all
wandering loose.
When I suddenly spotted, five car lengths away, a very
large, regal, male moose.
He stood very still at the edge of the wood; I was past him
in seconds, alas.
Through the mirror I saw him step royally out, cross the
road and step high through the grass.
With a sigh I continued, I'd missed such a shot, so I slowed
to much less than the limit.
Traffic was sparse, I was doing no harm and my chances
improved every minute.
Then ahead on the shoulder appeared a large heap. Was it
road kill? I just couldn't see.
I slowed even more just in case it was alive. Then it moved.
A big head looked at me.
"It's my bear!" I rejoiced as I slowed to a crawl, and took a
quick snap from the car.

It started to rise and my heart gave a leap t'was the biggest
bear I'd seen by far.
He rose slowly up, until on all fours, then ambled along on
the berm.
One hand on the wheel and camera in hand my driving
was surely not firm.
With one eye on the road, there was nothing about, except
me and that lumbering bear,
I daringly reached 'cross the passenger seat and took one
last snap from quite near.
And then I kept going, slowly at first, not wishing to startle
the lumberer,
And as I kept driving I yelled "Yes!" right out loud, I'd a
Yukon bear in my camera.
Much later, back home when I printed those shots I had
yet another surprise.
It wasn't the black bear I'd thought all along, but a large
grizzly bear met my eyes.
Today, looking back at that high in my life, I'm astonished
that I felt no fear.
And I'm thankful I sensibly stayed in the car and didn't get
close to that bear.

Sugaring Off

by Norma Beers

I shall rise up and go to the maple sugar trails
To the log cabin where we sugared each spring.
Brother Karl and I helped Grandpa tap and hang shiny sap
 pails.
With the wonderful scent of boiling sap permeating the air,
We raced to the warm cabin as if on a wing.

There, Grandma had supper on the fry
Ham, fresh bread, hash and corn.
For dessert a deliciously sweet maple sugar pie
Then we bedded down in the loft above
Til another early morn.

Daylight and the jingle of horses' bells
Made us jump from bed
Telling us Grandpa was already working on the day ahead.

Each spring Dad hired mill help for a sugaring date
Karl and I prepared fresh snow outside for the meet.
Grandpa whittled new wood paddles each night after we ate

I returned years later to the cabin in the woods.
To my horror it was occupied by a band of porcupine.

In the cabin, ceiling high, a pile of porcupine dung stood.
I retreated quickly, not even trying to establish my line
Knowing nature had retrieved what was no longer mine.

Misty October Morning

by Sylvia Findlay

I step out on an autumn morning into
nature's misty gauze.
Soon it will be All Hallow's Eve and I wonder
if the somber vapor is a ghost's grave-clothes?
Through chilly leaf strewn foggy streets
I hasten to my sylvan cathedral for comfort and renewal
whilst the sun appears as an opalescent moon.
Overhead invisible flocks of geese honk
their plaintive song,
a cacophony in the mist.
Are they lost, confused?
Stealthily I cross the footbridge;
startled, a great blue heron rises majestically,
the prehistoric creature's ashen wings make no sound.
Trees stand naked save the oak in her russet gown,
and the aspen, not parted from her frock
of green and yellow shimmer,
styled smartly against her stamped white trunk.
Migrating song birds trill their various notes
with brave abandon, made courageous
by the concealment of nature's misty curtain.
Satiated, I exit my cathedral, turn for home.
The sun, still an opalescent moon, hangs higher
in the dove gray sky of a ghost's grave clothes.

Snow Thoughts

by Janet Beers

Each magical flake
Swirls, ascends, accumulates
Into a perfect oneness
Landing gently on
A child's tongue
A pony's nose
A child's grave,
A lover's tear,
Slipping and sliding
It joins others to create
Snow
That amorphous part of our psyche.
Flake on flake blending, forming
An unbelievable pallet of white.
Affluent urban dwellers see it as a
Cleansing,
fun making

Shoveling, exhilarating,
Signal of our seasons.
Swathed in heaters and humidifiers
We revel in our different seasons.
Flex our muscles, or lack thereof,
On slopes or rinks,
Brag of fractures and aches
Caused by a distant call to be
Rocket Richard, Barbara Ann Scott,
Wayne Gretsky or Ross Pagliatti.
Just for a second
Before we slip into old age and spectatorism
We're Couriers de Bois Just one more time!

A Simple Chinese Woman

by May Albee

I am but a simple Chinese woman
No claim to fame have I
Brought up as Christian
In a far off desolate land
Never been baptized during
The Cultural Revolution time

Accompanying my daughter
To study for her Masters Degree in Computers
I landed in Canada
Now I go to Church whenever I can manage
Lending a helping hand
Sharing a simple lunch with a bunch

There I met a Chinese school teacher
Who showed me the future
Of teaching Chinese to children
With no English but plenty of ease
I combine the methods of the east
With the west

I learn their special strengths
From casual chatting
I praise them with a lot of love and patting
No combatting
Not long after
They try harder

I am but a simple Chinese woman
A grandmother to some
A favorite teacher to many with years to come.

The Learning Hive (Of Chariots Bonkers and Konkers)

by Kevin Delaney

Somewhere just past ten it came alive
A yard full of children spilling fresh out from the learning hive
Holding coat tails or belt loops in teams of two, three, four, and five
Thrashing and dashing about proving that both mind and body need to strive

Dutch-ie, Coloured-ie, Pure-ie Bonkers
Were part of the calls of the marble game hawkers
Pots-ies and Pings-ies with cat's eyes were played
While the marble-less gawkers gazed

Baked dry mahogany coloured nuts with a hardened glaze
Threaded on knotted strings one prays
Will win all the battles of that days play
And live to fight another day

Cries of 'hit one will get you five' call out as the teacher's bell comes alive
The sound of the bell connecting with clanger stops all in mid stride
Motionless statues await the command that orders chaos into lines
All over the yard near silent bodies form up to re-enter the learning hive

HAUNTING MEMORIES

by Sylvia Findlay

Captured in my memory is the ghost of a faded white,
 one-room, country school house.
Buffeted by winds, desolate, lonely and forlorn
 Wheatfield School waits for children
 who will never return.
Amidst the rolling prairie, no trees to shade
 the school in summer, constant unfettered winds
 swish prairie grasses, wild oats and tansy.
Meadowlarks sing from fence posts; undisturbed,
 gophers burrow under the doorstep, finding shade.
Blue bottle flies struggle to escape through
 dust-laden windows.
Swooping, gliding barn swallows
 leave the haven of the dilapidated outhouse
 to feast on buzzing insects.
Through the passage of time a long forgotten unmarked
 grave site, guarded by a sagging string of barbed wire,
 abides a lone companion to the school.
Cultivated fields leave no shelter or protection in winter.
Howling winds blow and drift, swirling and heaping
 fine dry snow into rock-hard banks and canyons.
The porch door faces south attempting to discourage
 the bitter north wind blowing snow indoors.
Heavily frosted windows, battered by storms,
 admit the winter sun.

Aromas of oil-soaked wood floors and dust
    hang over the room.
A portrait of King George VI and Queen Elizabeth
    gazes down from its lofty place.
On the blackboard below the regal couple,
    the cursive alphabet
    in lower and uppercase letters is displayed.
The teacher's desk, holding the summoning school bell
    and the dreaded strap,
    is in its rightful place at the head of the room.
Covered with silt, two rows of jackknife initialled,
    ink-stained desks sit empty.
Bereft coat hooks wait patiently.
Towards the back of the schoolroom stands
    a wood-burning space heater
    like a sentinel on guard.
Rusted and shabby, it appears innocuous,
    denying its former reputation.
Volatile, unpredictable and mean-tempered,
    it had demanded constant attention.
Occasionally, red hot, smoking furiously,
    scorching eyes and throat,
    it erupted into chimney fires, spreading
    panic amongst the youthful teacher and children.
Behind the bad-tempered heater, a glass-door bookcase
    contains ancient yellowed tomes of classics,
    mostly Dickens.
In the southeast corner stands a hand wound gramophone,
    boasting a total collection of six worn 78 rpm records.
Should I play 'The William Tell Overture' or

'Barney Google with the Goo-Goo-Googly Eyes?'
    I have a choice.
But now, if I listen closely; I may hear
    the tremulous voices of long-grown children echo
    throughout the rafters.
Laughter, recitations, carols and 'God Save the King,
    weave and waft above the whine of the wind.
Outdoors, hawks hunt, mice hide
    and the unrelenting prairie wind continues to blow.
Ropes rattling, pulleys clanking,
    a phantom Union Jack flaps from the flag post
    of a country school-house, saluting an era
    which is no more.

Rook Island Lighthouse

by Caroline O'Leary-Hartwick

Pretty in red and white it stands upon a solitary rock
With automatic light in hand
Where once only lighthouse keepers tread
Grandfathers, uncles, aunts and cousins too
All played their part
On the Rook Island lighthouse in the Chedabucto Bay

To the Queensport harbour they all came
Tall ships, to the lowly dory
To the small fishermen's diesel, to dragger boats
To tanker ships, to pleasure boats
All protected by
The Rook Island lighthouse in the Chedabucto Bay

Its beacon shone brightly on villages all around
Day and night it stood a symbol of our daily lives
It held laughter, sadness, danger and courage
Still it stood proud
The Rook Island lighthouse in the Chedabucto Bay

Now, it stands, still proud but forlorn
Long gone are the lighthouse keepers and their folk
Now the birds nest, and raise their young
But still it stands for us all to admire
With automatic light in hand
The Rook Island lighthouse in the Chebabucto Bay

Biographies

Albee, May

An American Chinese who teaches biology at various universities, May Albee wrote her poem on behalf of Ms. Zhibao Huang, 66 years old and a teacher at Xin Hua Chinese School in Ottawa, Ontario where her daughter presently attends.

Amyotte, Margaret

Margaret Amyotte presently lives in Ottawa, Ontario.

Azad, Mina

Mina Azad is a retired software designer. She was born and lived in Iran until age 22 when she went to the US for her graduate studies in computer engineering. She immigrated to Canada in 1980. She now lives in Ottawa, Ontario.

Beers, Janet

Janet Beers was born in 1944 in Halifax, Nova Scotia. She is now a retired high school English teacher and resides in Ottawa, Ontario.

Beers, Norma

Born in 1919 in Sherbrooke, Quebec. Norma Beers is now a retired elementary school teacher and presently resides in Ottawa, Ontario.

Braeuel, Giselle

Giselle Braeuel was born in the early 1930s and grew up in Volmarstein, Germany, during WW II. Since she immigrated to Canada in 1956, she has written quite a bit, published some poetry and even a small book about growing up during WW II. She now resides in Kanata, Ontario.

Casselman, Gail

Born in 1938 in Williamsburg, Ontario, Gail Casselman now lives in Ottawa, Ontario. She started her career as a primary school teacher and then became a stay at home mother for about fifteen years. When all the children were school age, she took an Office Administration course via a back to work program. She then worked on contract for various Government Departments for several years and then worked with CMHC for about nine years. She ended up as a records management clerk in the City of Ottawa Legal Branch and retired in 1998.

Chow, Sherman

Born in Shanghai, China, Sherman Chow came to Ottawa with his parents to Ottawa as an eleven year old boy in 1946. He was employed as an engineer at a Canadian Government telecommunications research laboratory until he retired in 1995. Sherman and his wife presently reside in Kanata, Ontario.

Delaney, Kevin

Kevin Delaney has arrived at that time of life that permits him the freedom to remember or forget as he sees fit. Life has been lived across Canada over some 60 plus years. Travel has taken him from Jakarta to Moscow; from Ottawa to Nicosia and may places in between. The fun is in the remembering and the telling but never the same way twice. Kevin now resides in Ottawa, Ontario.

Devlin, Mary Etta

Mary Etta Devlin presently resides in Ottawa, Ontario.

Findlay, Sylvia

Sylvia Findlay was born in rural Manitoba in 1937. A childhood of daily exposure to nature and her Ukrainian background has instilled an appreciation of her surroundings and heritage. She enjoys writing as a hobby, a recently developed pursuit. She has made her home in Ottawa for more than four decades but frequent visits to the prairie reinforce her nostalgic memories.

Fulthorp Jubb, Joan

Joan Fulthorp Jubb is 75, and although she grew up out west, she now resides in Ottawa, Ontario.

Gardiner, Ida May

Ida May Cardinal joined the baby-boomers in their journey through the Canadian experience in 1954. Lucky to be a part of the generation that could do anything, regardless of gender, she worked for Bell Canada on the leading edge of technology for the years before she became a stay-at-home mom. Now bouncing into early retirement, she writes, paints and enjoys a good book.

Gauthier, Michèle

Michèle Gauthier is the daughter of Félix Gauthier from St. Irenée in the Charlevoix region of Quebec. Her father will turn 100 years old in August 2014 and she is writing his memoirs to honour him, his life and the Gauthier family history. She now resides with her son, Alexandre in Ottawa, Ontario.

Gillham, Skip

E.B. "Skip" Gillham grew up in Toronto and raised his family in the Niagara region of Southern Ontario. His experience aboard ship also aroused his curiosity about the fate of the many ships he had seen with his dad in the Pre-Seaway era so he began researching and eventually writing about the ships of the Great Lakes. This provided opportunities to contribute articles to historical journals, newspapers, corporate newsletters, books and, in recent years, marine related websites. He has written 62 books on shipping and seen thousands of his articles in print. So much of what followed in his life was directly or indirectly related to the events of the "Summer of 63" fulfilling a dream of being a Great Lakes sailor.

Knapp, Ruth

Ruth Knapp is a retired teacher who presently resides in Ottawa, Ontario.

Lewis, Dick

Dick Lewis was born in 1940 in Ottawa, ON. He is a semi-retired dermatologist. He now resides in Kamloops, British Columbia.

Lewis, Gerard

Gerard Lewis was in born 1949 in Ottawa, Ontario. He is a self-employed facilitator and counsellor. He continues to reside in Ottawa, Ontario.

Lytle, Earl

Born in Sudbury Ontario, Earl Lytle went to public school in Ottawa, Ontario, and high school in Sharbot Lake, Ontario. He is a graduate of Royal Roads and RMC Military Colleges and has a Graduate Diploma from Carleton University. He served with the Canadian Army and the Federal Public Service (NHW, PSC and EMR). He presently lives with his wife Tooke in Ottawa, Ontario.

MacTaggart, Ted

Ted MacTaggart was born in Winnipeg, Manitoba. He is a retired army Major. He presently resides in Ottawa, Ontario.

Mathieu, Carol

Carol Mathieu grew up in rural Ottawa and still lives in Ottawa, Ontario.

McClure Larsen, Paula

I was born on June 30th,1945 in Moncton, New Brunswick. I was the first born and we bought our first house in Riverview, New Brunswick across the river from Moncton when I was three-years-old. What a wonderful world that was! I guess you could say "a little piece of heaven". I went to a private Business College in Moncton and worked as a receptionist, bookkeeper, stenographer, payroll clerk at a large cookie factory. I had so wanted to be a Social Worker but I met Hans in High School and he was graduating that year so being young and silly, I figured I could start making money faster by taking this route. We were married on August 22,1964 and Hans left for Air Traffic Control School a year later and when he returned from Ottawa, they transferred us to Stephenville, Newfoundland for one year and we moved to Gander after that.

McRae, Colleen

After retirement at age 70, Colleen McRae joined a writing group, took up watercolour painting, became part of a book club, and continued to keep her hand in helping people, which reflects her careers as a social worker, entrepreneur of teaching soft skills to adults, and co-ordinator of a co-operative housing unit.

Nash, Nedra

Nedra Nash is the mother of a very "Canadian" family: an American mother, Australian father, daughter born in Canadian, son adopted from Vietnam. She turned Canook so he could have a passport. She presently resides in Ottawa, Ontario.

O'Leary Hartwick, Caroline

Being raised by her grandparents in rural Nova Scotia gave Caroline O'Leary Hartwick her roots and values. Being blessed with a creative mind and a passion to do many things led her in many different directions in her life. She is married and lives in Ottawa, Ontario, where she raised her children; writing these stories are a gift to her grandchildren to give them a sense of who they are and their Acadian beginnings.

O'Neill, Marilyn

Marilyn O'Neill presently resides in Ottawa, Ontario.

Richer, Peter

Peter Richer presently resides in Ottawa, Ontario.

Salvin, Bobby

Born in Penzance, Cornwall, England, Bobby Salvin came to Canada with her children and husband in 1957. They became citizens in 1967. They had four children, three sons and a daughter, Alan in Ottawa, Ian in Waterloo, Neil and his four children in Whitehorse and Lynn, her husband and daughter in Haines Junction. Sadly Jim died in 2002. She presently resides in Ottawa, Ontario.

Squance, George

George Squance was raised in Devon England and is a retired chief E.R.A. He presently resides in Ottawa, Ontario.

Standish, Dick

Dick Standish was born 1940 in Brampton, Ontario. He was the Manager of Parks, Trees and Sewers for the City of Ottawa for 25 years and is now retired. He presently resides in Ottawa, Ontario.

Stockwell, Patricia

Patricia Stockwell is a retired English teacher, a mother of two adult daughters and a proud grandmother of a seven year old granddaughter and a five year old grandson. She wrote and published a children's book, Tricks on Gramma, and is currently looking for a publisher for her self-help guide, Out of the Cave, a book about understanding mental health issues. She is a regular contributor to Senior Lifetimes Newspaper and writes a weekly blog titled mentalhealthchallenges@blogspot.ca

Taylor, Marcia

Marcia Taylor lives with her husband in Ashton, Ontario, on a hobby farm which has neither crops nor animals. Her older son Graham, who was autistic, died in 2010 at the age of 33.

Thomas Shaw, Douglas

Douglas Thomas Shaw was born in Liverpool, England in 1919. Passed away in 2002. He is father to Marilyn O'Neill who also contributed a story.

Tunis, Rosalie

Born in Montreal in 1938, Rosalie Tunis moved to Ottawa, Ontario in 1971. She had a career as a teacher, then became a stay at home mom. Later, she worked for the federal government for 17 years. Right now she loves the freedom to choose what activities she does or doesn't do.

Vincent, Christine

Born in Ottawa at Grace Hospital in 1953, Christine Vincent has lived in Ottawa, Ontario all her life. She worked as a security guard as well as being a stay at home mum. She has a love of crafts, volunteering and animals.

Walker, Kay

Kay Walker was born in August 1929 on a ranch in Alberta. She moved to Ottawa, Ontario in 1968 when her husband was elected to Parliament.

Wilson, Linda

At 66, Linda Wilson considers herself a young senior, so she would like to help out while she can. She really enjoys writing poetry which so far has been well received. As well, she has written a number of memoirs from her childhood in Nova Scotia. She now resides in Ottawa, Ontario.

How You Can Help

Sponsorship

HelpAge offers different sponsorship programs to support a grandparent, a victim of sexual violence, a retired advocate, or a member of a marginalized community. Click on any of the items below to learn more and donate to these people in need.

Sponsor a Grandparent

Older persons around the world are struggling to sustain themselves without sufficient food, medicine or resources. The *Sponsor a Grandparent* program serves over 800 seniors who are now living healthy lives with your support. In return for your sponsorship, you will receive a photo of your sponsored grandparent and details of their living conditions. You will also receive an update twice a year, keeping you in touch with your grandparent.

What's the impact of your donation?

- Your donation of $34 helps provide basic essentials like food, water, clothing, shelter and medicine.

- It helps to restore dignity and hope and to provide a grandparent the respect that they deserve.

Sponsor a Retired Advocate

In an extremely difficult and high risk setting, advocates for SOFEPADI, our local partner in The Democratic Republic of Congo, give their best to promote peace and justice, and to defend the rights of Congolese women. Many of these advocates have been threatened, several attacked, and have come under pressure from the local authorities and/or their communities. Once they become too old to work, they find themselves alone, without a pension or support. In exchange for their testimonies, which help inform the greater public about the plight of many Congolese women and their communities, we provide retired advocates in the Democratic Republic of Congo with a monthly pension.

What's the impact of your donation?

- A monthly income is provided to a retired advocate who has spent years helping women, their families and communities that are at risk.

- It contributes to basic needs such as food, medication, clothing and shelter.

Income-Generating Activities

Affected by poverty, a lot of older persons in Kenya are abandoned by their families, forcing them to join the destitute population in urban slums. They have limited capacity to generate income and in some cases, living with or caring for those affected by HIV/AIDS generates additional challenges. ***HelpAge*** Canada supports income generating activities in Ahero Townships, Kenya, and Béni and Oicha in the Democratic Republic of Congo. Your donation will help impoverished older women and men and provide them with the means to make a living.

What's the impact of your donation?

- Your donation will contribute to food security and will provide a sense of self-worth and dignity to older persons.

Sponsoring a Victim of Sexual Violence

In the eastern Democratic Republic of Congo (DRC), women of all ages face threats from rebel groups, armed militias and sometimes the military or police. Women, young and old, continue to be victims of sexual violence in situations of armed conflict and instability. Attacks are common and access to medical and psychological support is extremely limited. Victims of sexual violence are often too afraid to seek treatment and can be shunned by their community and their families as a result of these horrific experiences. Victimized women emphasize the need for programs such as job-skills training with micro-loans to support their economic, physical and mental well-being.

What's the impact of your donation?

- Women who earn more are more likely to save for the future, promoting stability and improving the quality of life for themselves and their families

Sponsor an Older Person belonging to a Marginalized Community

The poorest communities in almost any region tend to be minority groups that have been targets of long-standing discrimination, exclusion and sometimes violence. The dire situation faced by many ethnic, religious or linguistic minorities is often made worse by discrimination and inequality. They are often denied equal access to quality education or have limited employment possibilities. This is the situation of the Pygmies in DR Congo, especially the Twa community in North Kivu.

What's the impact of your donation?

- Your monthly donation of $34 contributes to providing basic essentials such as food, shelter, medicine and clothing for an older person in the community.

Emergency & Reconstruction

Older men and women are some of the most vulnerable victims of disasters and conflicts. They face specific threats from man-made or natural disasters and their needs are very different from those of other age groups.

In collaboration with ***HelpAge*** International, a leading provider of humanitarian relief for older persons, and our local partners, we ensure that older persons are not forgotten in long-term humanitarian efforts.

What's the impact of your donation?

- Depending on what is needed, we work with other humanitarian aid providers to meet the needs of older persons. For example, in Haiti we provided funding to ***HelpAge*** International for the rebuilding of houses that are now hurricane resistant

- Older age means reduced mobility and muscle strength, impaired sight and hearing, and greater vulnerability to extreme weathers. Older persons also need healthcare for chronic conditions, such as coronary heart disease, diabetes, strokes, respiratory illnesses, rheumatism and dementia.